A Multimodal Stylistic Approach to Screen Adaptations of the Work of Alice Munro

This volume brings together perspectives from multimodal stylistics and adaptation studies for a unified theoretical analysis of adaptations of the work of Alice Munro, demonstrating the affordances of the approach in furthering interdisciplinary research at the intersection of these fields.

The book considers films and television programmes as complex multimodal stylistic systems in and of themselves in order to pave the way for a clearer understanding of screen adaptations as expressions of modal, medial, and aesthetic change. In focusing on Munro, Francesconi draws attention to a writer whose body of work has been adapted widely across television and film for an international market over several decades, offering a diachronic overview and insights into the confluence of socio-cultural contexts, audiences, and dynamics of production and distribution across adaptations. The volume complements this perspective with a microanalysis of the adaptations themselves, exploring the varied creative use of audio-visual dimensions, including sound, light, and movement. The book seeks to overcome simplified fidelity-based understandings of screen adaptations more broadly, showcasing creative multi-layered approaches to a creator's oeuvre to effect true transformation across media and modes.

The volume will be of interest to scholars in multimodality, adaptation studies, film studies, and comparative literature.

Sabrina Francesconi is Associate Professor of English Linguistics at the University of Trento. Her research interests are tourism and heritage discourses, adaptation studies, Canadian studies, humour studies, multimodal analysis, multimodal genre analysis, multimodal stylistics, and systemic-functional stylistics.

Routledge Studies in Multimodality
Edited by Kay L. O'Halloran, Curtin University

For more information about this series, please visit: https://www.routledge
.com/Routledge-Studies-in-Multimodality/book-series/RSMM

A Multimodal Stylistic Approach to Screen Adaptations of the Work of Alice Munro

Sabrina Francesconi

Routledge
Taylor & Francis Group

NEW YORK AND LONDON

First published 2023
by Routledge
605 Third Avenue, New York, NY 10158

and by Routledge
4 Park Square, Milton Park, Abingdon, Oxon, OX14 4RN

Routledge is an imprint of the Taylor & Francis Group, an informa business

Library of Congress Cataloging-in-Publication Data
Names: Francesconi, Sabrina, author.
Title: A multimodal stylistic approach to screen adaptations of
the work of Alice Munro / Sabrina Francesconi.
Description: New York : Routledge, 2023. | Includes
bibliographical references and index. |
Identifiers: LCCN 2022045809 (print) | LCCN 2022045810
(ebook) | ISBN 9781032025476 (hardback) | ISBN
9781003183846 (ebook)
Subjects: LCSH: Munro, Alice, 1931—Adaptations. | Munro,
Alice, 1931—Film adaptations. | Munro, Alice, 1931—Television
adaptations.
Classification: LCC PR9199.3.M8 Z625 2023 (print) | LCC
PR9199.3.M8 (ebook) | DDC 813/.54—dc23/eng/20221127
LC record available at https://lccn.loc.gov/2022045809
LC ebook record available at https://lccn.loc.gov/2022045810

ISBN: 978-1-032-02547-6 (hbk)
ISBN: 978-1-032-02552-0 (pbk)
ISBN: 978-1-003-18384-6 (ebk)

DOI: 10.4324/9781003183846

Typeset in Times New Roman
by codeMantra

Contents

Introduction

Adapting Clothes, Peaches, and Stories

Alice Munro has never been involved in the film adaptations of her works and has often admitted to not being interested in them (Alter 2014). Given the mediatic visibility and the financial profits the adaptation industry gives to adapted authors, the short-story writer's distance from her screen adaptations is surprising, and cannot be simply ascribed to lack of curiosity or to a reserved attitude. Munro's case is indeed exceptional, as many artists participate in the adaptation process to various degrees, operating as screenplay writers, consultants, or screenplay committee members. Authorial engagement, however, seems to imply a form of authorial control: it may prevent the aesthetic transformation inherent in the adaptation phenomenon. Hence, difference and distance in authorship, perspective, agency—alongside medial, modal, and contextual mutation—is part of the meaning-making adaptation process. I believe that screen adaptations of Munro's stories deserve inspection precisely because (and not in spite) of the writer's lack of involvement, since the personal, aesthetic, and critical detachment of the literary author enables the adaptation process to unfold in its most interesting form(s).

Not only has Munro's restraint from the phenomenon allowed the transcodifications of her stories to grow and travel. It has also enabled the story of her adaptations to develop along unpredictable trajectories. As the second part of the introduction will show, the initial stage of Munro's screen adaptations was a merely Canadian phenomenon (the author was born in Wingham, Ontario, in 1931), while it later expanded towards a more international horizon. Through the decades, the adaptation process has indeed crossed national borders and has embraced different countries, languages, and cultural systems. Moreover, adaptations have been significantly

DOI: 10.4324/9781003183846-1

affected by marketing, financial, and legal dynamics, proper to the adaptation industry. Meanwhile, different artists have been involved, including directors, screenwriters, composers, each one with their own distinct perspectives, competences, and toolkits. Resulting from multifaceted diachronic phenomena, all these film adaptation instances have variously changed the characters, plot, structure, tone, and motifs.

A further reason why film adaptations of Munro's works should be critically addressed is a thematic one: the Canadian author's stories obsessively narrate processes of adaptation. Her characters are often captured while adapting tangible or intangible materials like cloths or fruit, or when undergoing physical or mental processes of adaptation, especially in relation to storytelling. This phenomenon is also true of the narrators, who are engaged in ceaseless adaptation of narrative material, conceived as adaptable in structure, perspective, and style. Adaptation has, ultimately, affected the short-story form, which has mutated across the years and the editorial stages. Central to Munro's short stories and to Munro's writing process, the motif of adaptation will be discussed in this introduction, alongside its multifold and multifaceted implicatures.

Within the pages, adaptation is often thematised as a purposeful transformation, as a voluntary adjustment of products to new conditions and needs. Generally, this is a female art and often it affects dresses. The protagonist of "A Wilderness Station", Annie, is a seamstress and a storyteller, who deftly adapts clothes and stories: "[T]he dress Old Annie was wearing underneath was of plum-coloured silk. In fact, it was made over from the one she had made for my grandmother to meet the Prince of Wales in" (Munro 1995, p. 219).[1] Annie had, first of all, made a dress for the narrator's grandmother and for a special occasion and, then, had adapted ("made over") the same dress for herself. What remains is the material ("silk") and the colour ("plum"), while the size and shape change. In the story "Post and Beam", Polly makes the wedding dress for her younger cousin Lorna, adapting "her own high-school formal", putting "in gussets of white lace", and sewing "on white lace sleeves" (Munro 2002, p. 201). Lorna had meant to use her navy suit, but, some days before the ceremony, Polly had decided that it was not appropriate for the occasion and had worked on her own dress, by adding ("putting in") and integrating ("sewing") items. Similarly, in "Boys and Girls", the eleven-year-old narrator describes a coat her little brother is wearing: "[Laird] was wearing a little bulky brown and white checked coat, made down from one of mine" (Munro 1997, pp. 124, 125). Adaptation, in this case, consists in size reduction, as the piece of cloth owned by the protagonist is adapted to fit the brother's body and protect him from the cold.

Alongside dresses, food is a frequent target of change. "Boys and Girls" narrates how perishable fruit and vegetables are transformed into ("made into") durable products to feed the family during the wintertime:

> These days our back porch was piled with baskets of peaches and grapes and pears, bought in town, and onions and tomatoes and cucumbers grown at home, all waiting to be made into jelly and jam and preserves, pickles and chilli sauce.
>
> (Munro 1997, p. 118)

Like Laird's coat, the family's "jelly and jam and preserves, pickles and chilli sauce" result from a process of adaptation. Again, the agent is the mother, the one who adjusts clothes and who processes food to address the different environmental conditions and changing needs of her family. Something similar is narrated in "Soon", with a focus on raspberries being transformed (turned out) into jam: "There was more to be sold than fresh vegetables and berries. Jam, bottled juice, relish, were turned out in the kitchen. The first morning of Juliet's visit, raspberry-jam making was in the progress" (Munro 2006, p. 95). The preserves are to be sold for economic reasons, to contribute to Juliet's limited family income.

Elsewhere, adaptation is deployed as a cognitive and artistic process, in relation to the practice of storytelling. Munro's characters do not conceive of it as a means but as an end in itself; they experience pleasure in adaptation. In "Soon", Juliet loves indulging in retelling stories:

> The roof was steeply pitched, so that you could walk around in the middle of the attic. Juliet used to do that, when she was a child. She walked around telling herself some story she had read, with certain additions or alterations.
>
> (Munro 2006, p. 97)

Some characters like retelling stories they know with more negative traits, like in "Friend of my Youth", where the narrator confesses her wish to rewrite a story her mother used to tell: she would turn a noble figure into an oblique one. In "Silence", negative tints are adopted to rewrite story endings, as when Juliet hears the story of Charicleia in the theatre piece by Heliodorus, *Aethiopica*. The Queen of Ethiopia's white baby girl undergoes unlucky and dangerous events. When she risks being sacrificed by her own father, she is yet rescued. "Devising a different ending", Juliet plans to make Charicleia search for her mother, but to meet endless obstacles (Munro 2006, p. 152).

Present within Munro's stories, adaptation is also pervasive in her writing practice. The Canadian laureate admits (1996, p. x) she loves "working around the different ways of telling [a story]". Diegetic fragments and patterns are woven over and over across the narratives, like the ones about the onset of maternal illness. Munro's mother Ann Laidlaw was affected by Parkinson's disease. The tremor of the hand, the stiffness of the mouth, the rolling upwards of the eyes have been represented several times across her stories, including "The Peace of Utrecht", "The Ottawa Valley", "Winter Wind". The symptoms are associated with the daughter's embarrassment for what she perceived, age nine, to be theatrical and melodramatic behaviour. Repetitiveness is something Munro herself was frequently blamed for: when her third collection was published, *Globe and Mail* journalist William French asked (1974, p. 32) how long she could continue writing on the same themes. He failed to understand that what has always interested the author is the narrative tension between repetition and variation.

Albeit Munro rewrites all passages, sentences, and words in order to explore different ways of telling her stories, endings are a preferred target of narrative transformation. She admits to having changed and sometimes omitted conclusions, when she read her stories aloud in public (Struthers 1983). In her Nobel acceptance speech, the author remembers loving, as a child, *The Little Mermaid* by Christian Andersen. Yet, she found the story "dreadfully sad", because the prince, although profoundly in love, could not marry his beloved mermaid. Munro decided that, after all her pains, the protagonist needed a happy ending and she created one, only for herself: "it slipped my mind that it was only made up to be a different story for me". It seemed to her that the positive ending was the destiny of Andersen's story, what the story really deserved. The child's craving for a happy ending later mutated into a passion for the violent and tragic, after she discovered Charlotte Brontë, as Flora and Charicleia's stories testify to (Ross 1992; Thacker 2011).

In various literary passages, reference is made to the way the Canadian writer perceives her work, as hearing and grasping anecdotes, gossip, fragments from everyday situations, that can then be transformed into stories. In "Family Furnishings", the first-person narrator admits: "the work I wanted to do […] seemed more like grabbing something out of the air than constructing stories" (Munro 2002, p. 119). Story writing would, thus, be a mutation from the oral into the written form, from an elusive to a more stable entity, and from a fragmentary to a cohesive composition. As a matter of fact, Munro's style carries the traces of its original material, in its fractured nature, right-dislocations, reformulations, conversational tone, as if lacking advance planning and subsequent editing.

Not only does adaptation operate in the writer's approach towards her material but also towards the short-story form. If the recipient of the 2013 Nobel prize for literature as "the master of the contemporary short story" has exclusively devoted her career to the text genre with fourteen short-story collections, she has never pursued the formulaic or paradigmatic narrative configuration. Quite the opposite, as Howells sustains (1998, p. 9), "Munro has continued to experiment within the short story form", questioning and revising its aesthetics. Over the decades, stories have indeed become longer, entangled, elusive; style has transformed in search of tension, detachment, ellipsis; narrators have mutated into unstable, unreliable, fluid stances; genre borders have been challenged through mirror stories, trilogies, interconnected stories across an entire volume. To outline such fluid horizon, following is the list of Munro's collections:

- *Dance of the Happy Shades* (1968)
- *Lives of Girls and Women* (1971)
- *Something I've Been Meaning to Tell You* (1974)
- *Who do You Think You Are?* (1977)
- *The Moons of Jupiter* (1982)
- *The Progress of Love* (1986)
- *Friend of My Youth* (1990)
- *Open Secrets* (1994)
- *The Love of a Good Woman* (1998)
- *Hateship, Friendship, Courtship, Loveship, Marriage* (2001)
- *Runaway* (2004)
- *The View from Castle Rock* (2006)
- *Too Much Happiness* (2009)
- *Dear Life* (2012)

In Munro's stories and aesthetics, the multifaceted motif, theme, and trope of adaptation recall the meaning of evolution. It is not by chance that the metaphor of adaptation used in text transcodification is borrowed from the biological world, where it evokes natural intransitive processes of adjustment affecting plants and animals. Biological adaptation may refer to the transformation of life forms to suit mutated weather conditions: the decreasing of temperatures, the falling of snow, the shortening of days, the freezing of waters. The phenomenon may be either progressive and linear, or cyclic and rhythmic. In the latter form, it evokes the myth of Persephone, who inhabits the realm of the dead for one season and can return to the upperworld for the next season. The narrator of "The Peace of Utrecht" remarks that old and frail inhabitants cannot survive the rigid winter temperatures:

> The life in Jubilee is primitively seasonal. Deaths occur in the winter; marriages are celebrated in the summer. There is good reason for this; the winters are long and full of hardship and the old and weak cannot always get through them.
>
> (Munro 1997, p. 196)

In this light, adaptation is imbued with a connotation of survival.

The contact zone between adaptation and survival is located by McGill (2008, p. 98) along a Canadian national horizon. Arguing that adaptation is a pervasive theme in Canadian literature at large, McGill speculates about giving Atwood's cornerstone 1972 volume *Survival* an alternative title: *Adaptation*. Atwood identified survival as the main symbol of Canadian literature and of Canada at large. It may refer to "hanging on, staying alive" (Atwood 1972, p. 33) in the face of physical and cultural obstacles, including the land, the climate, cultural and political imperialism. Among the many forms and stages of the "victim position" aimed at survival Atwood illustrated, McGill, for his argument, specifically underscored the fourth "creative non-victim position", whereby one reacts in a positive and creative way to the surrounding dangers. Adaptation as survival, McGill argues (2008, p. 99), is also to be regarded within a broader process of "the formation and understanding of national culture". This includes identification as Canadian and distinction from the outside, generally from the US neighbour. The chapters in this volume will seek to show that screen adaptations of Munro tend to move along this cline, with a progressive movement towards creative transformation.

A Panoramic Shot over Adaptations

This section is meant to trace a panoramic shot over film and television adaptations of Munro's stories released over the last decades in

Canada and abroad. While the following chapters will concentrate on "the adaptation of Munro's stories", the main concern here are "the stories of adaptation of Munro's stories", involving identity, culture, nationality issues, as well as institutional, financial, and legal dynamics. Initially produced and delivered at a national level, adaptations of Munro's stories have indeed progressively achieved an international dimension, where they have been the expression of different and diverse socio-cultural systems. Following is a list of film and TV adaptations:

* *The Ottawa Valley* (1974) Dir. J. Manatis, Canadian Broadcasting Corporation TV
* *The Play's the Thing* (1974) Dir. R. Herb, Sunrise Films, TV Series, S. 1, Ep. 1, January 17th
* *Thanks for the Ride* (1983) Dir. J. Harrison, National Film Board of Canada
* *Boys and Girls* (1983) Dir. D. McBrearty, Atlantis Films
* *Lives of Girls and Women* (1994) Dir. R. Wilson, Paragon Entertainment Corporation
* *Connection* (1986) Dir. W. König, Atlantis Films and National Film Board of Canada
* *Away from Her* (2006) Dir. S. Polley, Canada Simone Urdl *et al.*
* *Canaan* (2008) Dir. M. Haghighi, Hedayat Film Co.
* *Edge of Madness* (2002) Dir. A. Wheeler, Lions Gate Films
* *Hateship Loveship* (2013) Dir. L. Johnson, Cassian Elwes *et al.*
* *Julieta* (2016) Dir. P. Almodóvar, Warner Bros
* *Piano Lessons* (2017) Dir. M. Goldman, University of Toronto

So far, film and television adaptations have progressively involved eight out of fourteen collections—the most adapted one being the tenth volume *Hateship, Friendship, Courtship, Loveship, Marriage*, arguably the aesthetic peak of her art. Including a forthcoming film based on *Runaway*, the adaptation industry has regularly produced, since the 1970s, an average of three products released every decade. Films have generally addressed a single short story, except for three cases, when an entire collection (*Lives of Girls and Women*), a trilogy (from *Runaway*), and the first independent part of a double short story (from *The Moons of Jupiter*) were transposed.

Overall, a variety of directors and companies have shot and produced the transcodifications of Munro's stories. Interestingly, an author who has been criticised for being confined to female topics and regional writing has been often adapted by male and non-Canadian directors. Specifically, six adapters are female and eight are male; eight directors are Canadian, two are from the USA, two are European, one is Iranian-Canadian, and one is Australian. Seen from a diachronic perspective, early works have been mainly "made in Canada". Film production involved the Canadian Broadcasting Corporation Television, historically aimed at promoting a Canadian national culture, as distinct from the US cultural system. This socio-cultural project was also related to the technological goals of the National Government, in its 1949 policy for television development. After the preliminary stage, Canadian screen works engaged with the adapted literary texts in a more active way. Boasting an established global dimension, more recent films showcase different forms of transculturalisation, including and affecting soundtracks, dialogues, settings, and cultural references mentioned or displayed within the film narrative. By looking more specifically at distinct adaptations, the next sections will trace this trajectory.

The Play's the Thing by Roland Herb was released in 1974. Based on "How I Met My Husband" from Munro's *Something I've Been Meaning to Tell You* (1974), the story is set after the Second World War and tells of a naïve young woman, Edie, working for the Peebles family, who live out of town, near Chesley, Ontario. The fifteen-year-old hired girl falls in love with a pilot, Chris Watters, who is staying for a while next to the Peebles' property to offer plane rides for a fee. One day, an unattractive yet wealthy woman arrives, pretending to be the pilot's fiancée. Suddenly, Chris leaves without any notice, promising Edie to write her. Every single day from that moment on, the hired girl waits for the postman at the letterbox, in vain. She ends up marrying the postman himself, who believed Edie had been devotedly waiting for him. Starring Lynne Griffin (Edie), George Robertson (Chris), and Angela Clare (Mrs. Peebles), the film was included in a theatrical drama television series based on Canadian-written plays planned by the CBC-TV producer George Jonas (Thacker 2011, p. 238). The work, inspired by Munro's story, inaugurated the anthology *The Play's the Thing*, composed of one-hour episodes, and presented by Gordon Pinsent.

The second adaptation relates to the same collection, *Something I've Been Meaning to Tell You,* and is based on a short story entitled "The Ottawa Valley". A portrait of her mother's family, Munro's story narrates the onset of the mother's Parkinson's disease, giving attention to her bodily symptoms and on how the family perceived and reacted to the at-that-time-unknown condition.

The thirty-minute TV special maintained its original title and was broadcast as part of CBC's Sunday evening *Performance* block of programming. Directed by Janine Manatis (born in the USA, then a Toronto resident) and written by Anna Raiser, the TV adaptation starred Karen Austin as Lena, Kay Hawtray as Dodie, Karen Pearson as Young Beth, Ken Pogue as James, and Madeleine Sherwood as old Beth. Almost inaccessible outside the CBC archives, this film has been almost forgotten (Herz 2013).

Directed by the British Eric Till, the third TV adaptation was *1847: The Irish, The Newcomers/les arrivants.* This product should not be included in the present list, as it was not inspired by Munro's short stories. Broadcast on January 8, 1978, the seven-hour CBC miniseries was instead one of the Canadian author's few screen credits, edited by Charles Israel as *A Better Place than Home, The Newcomers: Inhabiting a New Land.* Written by Alice Munro and Timothy Findley, the episodes explored immigration to Canada. Featuring famous and appreciated actors including R.H. Thomson and Kenneth Welsh, the miniseries was successful at the time of its release. As Thacker claims (2011, p. 277), "Munro accepted these projects for further income, but they had the effect of extending her reputation beyond her readership".

Still "made in Canada" but outside the CBC context, a second group of audio-visual artefacts were produced by a private company in the first case, by a National Board in the second case, and by the cooperation of the two in the third case. The film *Boys and Girls*, directed by Don McBrearty and released in 1983, is based on the story of the same title, from the first collection by Munro, *Dance of the Happy Shades* (1968). Told by an unnamed, first-person narrator, the adapted text revolves around the everyday life of a family, who live in a farmhouse in a small-town Southwestern Ontario community and raise horses and foxes. The film foregrounds Margaret's personal growth, as she first defends, then challenges the paternal mindset. Starring Megan Follows as the protagonist Margaret, the twenty-five-minute adaptation was produced by the small Atlantis Films—which received the Academy Award as best story-live-action film (Thacker 2011, p. 407).

Written and directed by John Kent Harrison, the fifth adaptation of Munro's stories is *Thanks for the Ride* (1983) and also adapts a story collected in *Dance of the Happy Shades.* The main actors include Lesley Donaldson (Vicky), Melissa Bell (LoreAnn), Peter Kranz (George), and Carl Maroote (David). Produced by the National Film Board of Canada, the twenty-eight-minute short film focuses on a romantic double date that took place in the region on the shores of Lake Huron between two young men and two young women. The title refers to a cry by the female protagonist Vicky, which closes the film and challenges the leading role played by the male characters across the narrative. *Thanks for the Ride* provides some interesting solutions to the adaptation process, like the use of Sinatra's "Hello, young lovers" as a soundtrack.

Produced by Atlantis Films and the National Film Board of Canada, *Connection* (1986) was written by Kelly Rebar, directed by Wolf König, with music composed by Harry Freedman. The twenty-four-minute adaptation features Kate Trotter (Maureen), Patricia Hamilton (Iris), and Tom Butler (Richard). Set in Vancouver, it revolves around the relation between charming Maureen and her snobbish and rich husband Richard. When they receive a call from Iris, a cousin Maureen has not seen for a long time, Maureen invites her for dinner. Iris's joyful visit and her pleasant family stories visibly irritate Richard. After Iris's departure, Maureen's exasperation leads her to throw a plate of pie at her hostile husband. Collected in *The Moons of Jupiter* (1982), Munro's "Connection" is part of a double short story devoted to her family history, entitled "Chaddeleys & Flemings".

Also produced for the TV but by Paragon Entertainment Corporation, *Lives of Girls and Women* (1994) was directed by Ronald Wilson and written by Charles K. Pitts. The film was completed in 1994, but broadcast only in 1996, with actors including Tanya Allen as Del Jordan, Wendy Crewson as Ada Jordan, Peter Mac-Neil as Tom Jordan, and Amos Crawley as Owen Jordan. Written in the first-person, the work narrates the personal growth of a young woman, Del Jordan, as she navigates family tensions, spiritual and religious inquiries, as well as sentimental and sexual experiences. Published in 1971 as a novel, the adapted *Lives of Girls and Women* offers seven chapters and an epilogue, which can be better read as interconnected short stories. It is precisely the genre configuration of this work that posed the main challenges to screenwriter and director.

Governed by the aforementioned centrifugal force, the third group of works reveals its Canadian identity, yet takes on an international dimension. *Edge of Madness* is a mystery drama directed by Anne Wheeler (2002), written by Anne Wheeler and Charles K. Pitts, produced by Lions Gate Films (a US company, first established in Vancouver) and featuring Caroline Dhavernas, Brendan Fehr (Simon) and Corey Sevier (George). In the opening scene, a young woman reaches shelter, after walking across the snow-covered wilderness landscape. In front of a Clerk of the Peace, she confesses to the murder of her husband, Simon Herron. The ninety-five-minute film is based on the epistolary narrative "A Wilderness Station" from the eighth collection *Open Secrets* (1994), where a historian tries to recover the Southwestern Ontario pioneer past. Differently, Wheeler's film is set in 1851, along the Red River Valley, in a remote area of the Canadian Province of Manitoba. Curiously, what Herz (2013) defined: "Munro's first proper film adaptation" was distributed in theatres in Norway and Thailand, but was released only in DVD format in Canada.

A critically acclaimed adaptation is *Away from Her* (2006), directed and written by the Canadian artist Sarah Polley. Interpreted by Julie Christie and Gordon Pinsent (the *The Play's the Thing*'s presenter, Grant in this film), the film earned Oscar nominations for Polley's screenplay and Julie Christie's interpretation of Fiona. It brought to the screen "The Bear Came Over the Mountain" from *Hateship, Friendship, Courtship, Loveship, Marriage* (2001), a story about a seventy-year-old woman, Fiona, who develops a form of senile dementia. When symptoms become evident, Fiona is hospitalised in a specialised centre, where she establishes new social relations and falls in love with Audrey, also a patient. Interestingly, Polley works extensively at the cultural level, as she enhances references to Canadian culture within the narrative, from Canadian icons like the national flag or the Maple Leaf games, to pieces of Canadian literature like Alistair McCleod's novel or Michael Ondaatje's poem, to songs by the Canadian musician Neil Young.

The third film in this group is a later short film released in 2017, therefore temporally located in the last stage of Munro's work. However, *Piano Lessons* is a Canadian project and fully deserves a position here. The director and producer is Marlene Goldman, a writer, filmmaker, and English professor at the University of Toronto. Goldman is also the film's co-writer, together with Philip McKee. The soundtrack is by Chris Thornborrow, famous for composing the music for the award-winning film *Sleeping Giant*. Actors include Nancy Beatty, David Storch, Beatriz Yuste, and Rebecca Gregor. This fifteen-minute short film adapts Munro's "In Sight of the Lake", from Munro's last collection *Dear Life* (2012), and revolves around senile dementia, a topic Goldman has extensively and convincingly researched in her academic career. The leading character is Nancy, who is late for an appointment but has lost the address. She starts facing the onset of a strange and destabilising illness, accompanied by her caring granddaughter Alex. *Piano Lessons* has been supported by the Munro family and endorsed by the Alzheimer's Association of Canada.

The last group of adaptations signals the affirmed international dimension of films, both in terms of production and direction. The first example is *Canaan* (2008), an Iranian film by the Iranian-Canadian director Mani Haghighi, and based on "Post and Beam", once more from Munro's tenth collection. Produced by Hedayat Film Co, co-written by Mani Haghighi and Asghar Farhadi, *Canaan* features Mohammad Reza Forutan as Morteza, Taraneh Alidoosti as Mina, Afsaneh Bayegan as Azar, and Bahram Radan as Ali. Set in an exclusive and modern area in Tehran, the film tells the story of Mina who, after being married for ten years, decides to leave her husband Morteza. A few days before the divorce, which will give Mina the freedom to leave her country and moving to Canada, some events disrupt her plans. By the French-Iranian composer Christoph Rezai, the film's music profoundly contributes to the transcultural dimension of the adaptation, alongside setting, costume and dialogue.

Based on the epistolary story "Hateship, Friendship, Courtship, Loveship, Marriage" and directed by the American director Liza Johnson, *Hateship Loveship* was released in 2013. On the occasion of the premiere of the film, at the 2013 Toronto International Film Festival, the author admitted, through her editor Ann Close, that she had not seen the film and probably would never watch it: she did not think her comments would be useful (Alter 2014). Actors include Kristen Wiig as Johanna Parry, Guy Pearce as Ken, Hailee Steinfeld as Sabitha, and Nick Nolte as Mr. McCauley. Unlike Munro's story set in rural Ontario, the film was shot in Louisiana for financial reasons. The plot revolves around Johanna Parry, a reserved caregiver who starts working for rich and elderly Mr. McCauley and for his granddaughter Sabitha. Encouraged and supported by her friend, Sabitha organises a cruel joke on the housekeeper, sending her emails purportedly from Sabitha's father.

At the time of writing, the most famous screen adaptation of a story by Munro is *Julieta*, mainly in relation to the director's celebrity status. It was indeed the Spanish artist Pedro Almodóvar who based his film on a Trilogy collected in *Runaway* (2004). The protagonist is a middle-aged woman, abandoned by her daughter who avoids any contact with her mother and refuses to provide any explanation. This work had captured Almodóvar's attention and the future adapted film was anticipated by showing a copy of *Runaway* in a scene of a previous work, *In the Skin I Live in* (2011). Originally, the Spanish director had planned to shoot the film—to be entitled *Silence*—in the USA, in the English language, and Meryl Streep had accepted Juliet's role. Almodóvar later changed his mind: set the film in Spain (in Madrid, Galicia, and the Pyrenees); used the Spanish language; and chose two actresses, Adriana Uguarte as the young Julieta, and Emma Suárez as the adult protagonist. The film was presented at the Cannes film festival in 2016 and nominated for the Palme d'Or.

The last film of this fourth group and of the whole panoramic gaze is part of a still-in-progress Australian story and regards the adaptation of "Runaway", from the same 2004 volume. The film should be produced by Liz Watts and follow the story of Carla, who lives an unsatisfying and entrapping marriage, with her emotionally unstable husband, Clark.

Dissemination of Preliminary Results

This volume is the synthesis of an academic research project devoted to television and film adaptations of Munro's stories I have conducted across the last eight years. Preliminary results have been discussed in national and international conferences and disseminated in journal articles. The first two presentations I delivered were concerned with Pedro Almodóvar's screen adaptation of Juliet's Trilogy. The first was entitled "Juliet(a) across the Media" and was delivered at the *Made in Canada: The Languages of the Media* conference, held at the University of Naples "l'Orientale" in June 2016, while the second was entitled "Transmodal Crossings: Juliet from Page to Screen" and was presented at the *Transatlantic Crossing* Conference held by the University of Toulouse Jean-Jaurès in April 2017. More concerned with methodological issues was the presentation entitled "Challenging Approaches to Film Adaptation(s): *Boys and Girls* by Don McBrearty", delivered at the *Thinking Out of the Box in Language, Literature, Cultural and Translation Studies* conference, held by the Italian Association of English Studies at the University of Padova in September 2019. The following two papers address two significant tropes identified in the adaptions, namely letters and mirrors. The first was "Letters across Media and Modes: Film Adaptations of Alice Munro's Stories", delivered in December 2018 at conference of the Italian Association of Canadian Studies organised at the University of Trento, whereas the second was "Gender at the Mirror in Screen

Adaptations of Munro's Stories: A Multimodal Stylistic Analysis" at the *Intersezionalità e genere* conference held at the University of Naples "l'Orientale" in December 2019. The last paper, entitled: "Forms and Functions of the Voice-Over in Screen Adaptations", was concerned with socio-cultural issues and was delivered in July 2021 at the Poetics and Linguistics Association Annual Conference hosted by the University of Nottingham. Over the years, and across these stages of research, I have particularly focused on, improved, and honed my theoretical perspective on adaptation studies, methodological framework for multimodal stylistic analysis, and combined discussion of adapted texts and their film adaptations.

Alongside oral papers, preliminary results have been disseminated through written publications. Entitled "La traduzione intersemiotica: da 'The Bear Came over the Mountain' di Alice Munro a *Away from her* di Sara Polley", the first publication is collected in *Terminologia, Linguaggi specialistici, traduzione. Prospettive teoriche e pratiche* edited by Paola Faini (2018). A second article in the same year (2018) examines *Hateship Loveship* by Liza Johnson; it was published in the journal *Lingue e linguaggi* with the title: "'A sign of a letter coming': Adapting Munro's (Faked) Epistolary Correspondence". Published in the journal "Textus: English Studies in Italy" (2019) with the title "Film Adaptation as Intersemiotic Contact Zones: *Edge of Madness* by Anne Wheeler", a third article addresses the film adaptation *Edge of Madness* by Wheeler. In the same year, the article "Short-Film Adaptations of Munro's Stories in the 1980s: A Multimodal Stylistic Analysis" appeared in *Lingue e linguaggi*. Finally, the article "'Transparent Tricks': Looking in the Mirrors of Screen Adaptations" has been published in the volume *Adaptation of Stories and Stories of Adaptation: Media, Modes and Codes* (2020) I have co-edited with Gerardo Acerenza.

Volume Outline

The present volume includes one theoretical chapter, one methodological chapter, and three empirical chapters. Each of the latter chapters addresses three film adaptations, representative of the three main stages of the story of adaptation. The Introduction to the volume discusses the motif of adaptation in Munro's stories and its multifold and multifaceted implicatures. It then outlines the TV and film adaptations of her works, first released in Canada and then worldwide.

The first chapter outlines theories of adaptation developed across the last decades by scholars in the field. Accordingly, adaptation is addressed both as a product and as a process, and, in this second perspective, as a process of interpretation and creation. The chapter also illustrates the intertextuality of adaptation, in its aesthetic and political components, as it involves texts and people. It finally deals with modes and forms of involvement implied by an inclusive and open definition of adaptation, evoking the biological definition of adaptation as evolution, thus implying mutation.

The second chapter illustrates the methodology for the study, namely multimodal stylistics, as it developed across the last two decades, integrating stylistics and multimodality. It first presents stylistics as a composite field of enquiry, which addresses style as a variation of language use. It then focuses on multimodal stylistics, taken as a sub-field of stylistics, concerned with a range of modes and modal resources making meaning in a multimodal text. It finally shows how modes operate and integrate in screen adaptations. Specific attention is devoted to language, instantiated as voice-over, voice-in, and intertitles.

The third chapter focuses on three short films released in the 1980s in Canada: *Boys and Girls*, *Thanks for the Ride* and *Connection*. These films epitomise the first stage of screen adaptations of Munro's stories, developed within a national dimension, by three male directors, and with a limited duration of about twenty-five minutes. The multimodal stylistic analysis addresses strategies for expressing interiority, point of view and narrative stance in the audio-visual artefacts, as well as space.

The fourth chapter addresses a second stage of screen adaptations of Munro's stories, including more extended films, directed by directors in Canada: *Edge of Madness*, *Away from Her*, *Lives of Girls and Women*. This chapter is mainly concerned with strategies for shaping the temporal dimension in these three instances, in terms of (dis)continuity and in its implication for character, setting, and event representation.

The fifth and last chapter addresses the latest stage of screen adaptations of Munro's stories, which signal an established international dimension, in terms of production, direction, and fruition. Films include *Canaan*, *Julieta*, *Hateship Loveship*. Questions will be raised on how the films negotiate cross-cultural patterns and issues, in the migration from the Canadian to the Iranian, Spanish, and Australian cultural systems. The last section offers some concluding remarks.

Note

1 Short-story titles are in between quotation marks, whereas titles of short-story collections are in between italics.

References

Alter, A. (2014) Alice Munro's Prolific Film Career, *Wall Street Journal*, April 4th.

Atwood, M. (1972) *Survival: A Thematic Guide to Canadian Literature*, Toronto, Anansi.

French, W. (1974) Beautiful. Her Talent's Transportable, *Globe and Mail*, May 25th, 32.

Herz, B. (2013) Exploring Alice Munro, but Not through Her Books, *Maclean's*, October 10th.

Howells, C.A. (1998) *Alice Munro*, Manchester, Manchester U.P.

McGill, R. (2008) No Nation but Adaptation: The Bear Came over the Mountain, Away from Her, and What It Means to Be Faithful, *Canadian Literature/Littérature canadienne*, 197, pp. 98–111.

Munro, A. (1995) *Open Secrets*, London, Vintage.

Munro, A. (1996) *Selected Stories*, Toronto, Penguin.

Munro, A. (1997) *Dance of the Happy Shades*, Toronto, Penguin.

Munro, A. (2002) *Hateship, Friendship, Courtship, Loveship, Marriage*, New York, Knopf.

Munro, A. (2006) *Runaway*, London, Vintage, pp. 48–158.

Ross, C.S. (1992) *A Double Life: A Biography of Alice Munro*, Toronto, ECW Press.

Struthers, J.R. (1983) The Real Material: An Interview with Alice Munro, in L. MacKendrick (ed.) *Probable Fictions: Alice Munro's Narrative Acts*, Toronto, ECW, pp. 5–36.

Thacker, R. (2011) *Alice Munro: Writing Her Lives: A Biography*, Toronto, McClelland & Stewart.

1 Adaptation(s)

Towards a Definition

The *OED* provides interesting insights into the meaning "adaptation" had originally and the one it developed across the centuries. The oldest occurrence of the adjective "adapted" dates back to 1425, meaning "suitable, fitting", with reference to a specific use or purpose. The corresponding noun form "adaptation" signified the condition of "adaptedness, suitableness". Thus, the first usage indicated an "intrinsic and static essence" and an "innate suitability to a condition" (Jellenik 2017, p. 39). At the end of the eighteenth century, the meaning slightly changed and referred to the active transformation of an entity to suit new conditions and new functions; the term no longer identified a state, but a process. In the early Romantic period, adaptation steadily identified a process of mutation, a "productive possibility of change". Jellenik (2017, p. 37) does not find this surprising: the Romantic period was marked by notions such as genius, art, and originality on the one hand, but also of fluidity, change, and innovation on the other hand. Interestingly to this volume, the use of the term "adaptation" to indicate textual alteration dates back to the late eighteenth century.

The complex semantics raised by the term "adaptation" itself is reflected in the research devoted to the field of adaptation(s). Specifically, critical discussion upon film adaptations of literary works has a long tradition and encompasses a broad multidisciplinary and cross-disciplinary area at the crossroads of literary, media, and semiotic studies. Notable contributions have been offered by the disciplinary fields of comparative literature, literature and film, and English; film, media, and communication studies; translation studies, semiotics, and multimodal research. However, situating adaptation studies within disciplinary areas, Elliott argues (2014, p. 576), was a twentieth-century concern of scholars in the field,

DOI: 10.4324/9781003183846-2

while the twentieth-first century is involved in theoretical issues. Theories like postmodernity and poststructuralism, elsewhere established many years before, started being used later in adaptation studies, which experienced a "theoretical turn" only in the mid-1990s. The delay implied a polarisation of positions and the absence of integrated approaches (Elliott 2014, p. 576). In order to understand and contextualise this point, it is useful to cast a panoramic gaze upon the critical and academic debate upon adaptation(s). To this end, the following section relies on the four stages in adaptation studies outlined by Leitch in his introduction to the *Oxford Handbook of Adaptation Studies* (2017, p. 2ff).

The preliminary stage in adaptation studies is defined by Leitch as the prehistoric age and ended with the publication of George Bluestone's aesthetic formalist *Novels into Film* (1957). Called by Leitch "Adaptation studies 0.0" (2017, p. 2ff), this period anticipated adaptation studies proper. No studies in this time span overtly addressed adaptations; they rather considered, more generally, literature and films, their affordances and constraints, and their mutual relations. Texts included Virginia Woolf's 1926 essay "The cinema", which dismissed screen adaptations as minor and parasitic forms and sustained the impossibility of turning a complex novel like *Anna Karenina* into a film.

In the following 1.0 stage, adaptation studies became a field of enquiry and a method of analysis, starting from Bluestone's pioneering work. According to Leitch (2017, p. 2ff), "Adaptation studies 1.0" was primarily medium-based, concerned with exploring meaning-making strategies of adaptations derived from the filmic signifying system. The peak of the 1.0 stage in adaptation studies is the year 1996, when two ground-breaking books challenged the previously dominating methodologies of New Criticism and aesthetic formalism. The first is Brian McFarlane's *Novel to Film: An Introduction to the Theory of Adaptation*, aimed to promote structuralist narratology as a systematic, objective, and empirical approach towards adaptation, in opposition to subjective and impressionistic methodologies. The work provided a theoretical account of page-to-screen transformation, as well as a careful assessment of what constitutes "transferable" and "non-transferable elements" in adaptations. Transferable elements are not connected to the semiotic mode in which they appear and are called "narrative". Non-transferable elements are tightly tied to the system of signification of their manifestation and are called "enunciation". If narrative elements undergo a process of simple

transfer from the novel to the film, enunciation elements experience adaptation proper (McFarlane 1996, p. 20). In the same year,
Deborah Cartmell et al. (1996) published *Pulping Fictions: Consuming Culture across the Literature/Media Divide,* "the first of
many co-edited collection publications that brought left-wing politics and postmodern cultural theory into literature and film studies
with the force of the returning repressed" (Elliott 2014, p. 577). The
challenge to traditional theories was, in this second case, politically connoted, as low and popular culture was celebrated, alongside master narratives and grand theories. These two 1996 books
established what Elliott termed (2014) "the formal-cultural divide"
in adaptation studies, with formalists accusing cultural adaptation
scholars of lacking rigour and systematisation, and cultural scholars accusing adaptation formalists of conducting formulaic and
empty research.

Quite differently, the next stage of "Adaptation studies 2.0" (2017,
p. 2ff) revolves around the principle of intertextuality, drawing on
studies by Mikhail Bakhtin, Julia Kristeva, and Gérard Genette.
The core of the 2.0 period is, according to Leitch, Robert Stam's
three-book series, including 2005 *Literature and Film: A Guide to
the Theory and Practice of Film Adaptation,* whereby adaptations
are celebrated in their profound intertextual nature and politically
liberating impulse. Further influential works in the 2.0 age included
Deborah Cartmell and Imelda Whelehan's (1999) collection *Adaptation: From Text to Screen, Screen to Text.* The 2000s, Elliott
observes (2014, p. 581), marked the flourishing of cultural and contextual adaptation studies. A crucial contribution to this debate is
Linda Hutcheon's *A Theory of Adaptation* (2013 [2006]), where the
Canadian scholar reconceptualises adaptation, offering an open
and fluid definition, including a wide range of textual forms and
textual practices. Within a postmodern cultural theory of adaptation, she explores the telling and retelling of stories in adaptations
conceived as textual products, as well as in stories of adaptation,
where socio-cultural, economic, legal issues are at stake. Anchor-
ing the definition of adaptations in their reception, Hutcheon focuses on how adaptations derive from multifold interpretative and
creative practices, on how they variously engage audiences and
on how meaning-making is, accordingly, negotiated. In the 2000s
and 2010s, attempts have been made to resolve the formal-cultural
divide with a more inclusive, integrated, and synthetic approach,
giving birth to more hybrid studies. These can be inscribed into a
process of "reconciling the rifts" (Elliott 2014, p. 584), of finding

"ways to study adaptations holistically across formal-cultural and textual-contextual divides *amid* ideological disagreement".

The most recent age of "Adaptation studies 3.0" (Leitch 2017, p. 2ff) denounces the limits of intertextual studies for adaptation studies, and the risk of conflation and the absorption of adaptation studies by intertextual studies. In a leading stream of research, adaptations are explored also through notions such as intermediation and transmediation, whereby relations across media products and their implications in a wide range of communication situations are explored. From a synchronic perspective, different media can be examined in the combination and integration of media traits. From a diachronic perspective, the transfer and transformation across time of media products, media types and media traits are the object of inspection. Specifically, the paradigm of "transmedia storytelling" or "transmedia narrativity" describes narratives crossing different media types to form a broader narration and evoking "an old and widespread phenomenon that can be observed in, for instance, Hindu, Greek and Christian mythologies" (Elleström 2020, p. 6). In transmedia storytelling, different sections of the narrative are distributed in distinct media platforms. According to Elleström (2017, 2020), adaptation studies can profit significantly of the broader intermedial research context since adaptations, as actual or potential transfers among media, aptly epitomise the phenomenon of transmediation within the artistic domain (Elleström 2017, p. 512). Research in the 3.0 age devotes particular attention to digital technologies, to digital literacy, and to ceaseless and multiverse trajectories of digital storytelling.

Especially in its late stages, the contemporary critical debate upon adaptation(s) has been relying on several authoritative platforms. The Association of Adaptation Studies, based at De Monfort University, Leicester, with their Centre for Adaptations and their journal *Adaptation* (Oxford University Press) has been a particularly productive platform for interdisciplinary research on adaptation. Other relevant scientific journals are the *Journal of Adaptation in Film and Performance* (Intellectual Publications) and the *Literature/Film Quarterly*, founded in 1973 (Salisbury University). More recently, monographic volumes devoted to the adaptation of works by a given author, or to a given theme or phenomenon are being published in specialised editorial series such as Palgrave *Studies in Adaptation and Visual Culture*.

The definitions associated with the term and raised across the research stages have been informed by socio-cultural frames over the course of time. Overall, Corrigan observes (2017, p. 23) that three main perspectives on adaptation can be envisaged:

- adaptation as process
- adaptation as product
- adaptation as reception

In turn, these can be ascribed to three different models in various fields, domains, disciplines, including biology, technology, literature: evolution, fidelity, intertextuality. About sociological and biological forms of adaptation, the first is the broadest frame, whereby adaptation is perceived as an evolutionary process adapting to environmental or social conditions, in the Darwinian sense of "physical survival and advancement" (Corrigan 2017, p. 25). With a theological and mythological approach, the second meaning indicates the product of such transformation, and regards the adaptation of narratives and images with adaptations or transformations of ancient myths into contemporary variations. More recent and nourished by subjective and hermeneutic concerns, the third rhetorical and representational sense includes forms such as quotations, pastiche, and parodies. In this vein, adaptation is intended as intertextual relations enacted through reception, with a focus on meaning-making performed through reading and viewing (Corrigan 2017, p. 27). In light of this critical interdisciplinary discussion, the following sections explore the main approaches towards adaptation. The first is the discourse upon fidelity in adaptations and fidelity as a critical approach towards adaptations.

The Limits and Risks of Fidelity

Research in adaptation theory and practice often adopts the lens of "fidelity discourse" (Hutcheon, 2013; Leitch 2003; McFarlane 1996; Stam 2005). Accordingly, plot, setting, socio-cultural context, characters, dialogues should be equivalent in the two textual instances and the value of the adaptation would be proportional to its degree of faithfulness to its source text. To borrow examples from McFarlane (1996, p. 11), Peter Bogdanovich's *Daisy Miller* (1974) or James Ivory's *Howard's End* (1992) would be faithful adaptations, whereas *Sabotage* (1936) or *The Birds* (1963) by Alfred Hitchcock would be unfaithful films.

However, Leitch sustains (2003, p. 161) that fidelity discourse is "unattainable, undesirable, and theoretically possible only in a trivial sense". Looking for a faithful repetition of a source implies neglecting the ontological gap between two different texts as "the source texts will always be better at being themselves" (Leitch 2003, p. 161). Even "remakes in the same medium" cannot replicate the source text, given contextual conditions of codification and decodification (Leitch 2003, p. 161). If we were interested in the equivalence of the adapted text, for instance a literary text, we would better reread that literary text. Even in that case, though, we would neglect the fact that reading and rereading enact two distinct semiotic processes, as, while rereading, we would be familiar with the plot and the narrative resolution. In the case of screen adaptations, moreover, a fidelity approach would compare incomparable texts from an ontological reason, also because of medial and modal divergences. Aesthetic, semiotic, and technological differences are not only inevitable but also pivotal in adaptation as they motivate the existence of the adaptation itself.

Fidelity criticism is verbally expressed through morally driven vocabulary, with terms such as "contamination", "betrayal", "violation", "corruption", used to dismiss the adaptation change (Stam 2005, p. 54). By this, the inherent superiority of the source text is celebrated as authentic, and the inherent inferiority of the adapted text is condemned as inauthentic. The reasons for this prejudice, Stam argues (2005, p. 4), are also based on an "a priori valorisation of historical anteriority and seniority" as well as of the appreciation of origin and source as such. The bias also relies, as Stam elaborates upon (2005, p. 4), on a binary system of thought, which claims a "bitter rivalry between film and literature" and favours the second on the basis of iconophobia, logophilia, and an intellectual preference, dismissing a presumed popular and accessible dimension of the film. This attitude is not surprising, since academic interest in adaptations is generally shared among literary scholars, who tend to aprioristically prefer literary texts to cinematographic ones (Leitch 2003, p. 162; McFarlane 1996, p. 8).

From a fidelity lens, adaptations are not only seen as inferior but also as parasitic texts, namely deprived of an autonomous identity. Firmly arguing against the perception of adaptations as subsidiary forms, Hutcheon sustains that adaptations rely on "derivation that is not derivative" (2013, p. 9) and enact "repetition without replication" (2013, p. 7). In order to signal this kind of relation, she invites replacing terms such as "source text", "original text", and "originary text" with the term "adapted text", which avoids any hierarchal perception or organisation. The same term will be adopted here.

However, fidelity should not be totally dismissed in adaptation analysis; it may be better adopted as a non-exclusive parameter, as one criterion among others. McFarlane suggests avoiding general enquiries upon the adaptation's faithfulness to its "source" and invites problematising and deconstructing the tenet. The question to be raised, the Australian scholar observes (1996, p. 9), should be then "fidelity to what?", in relation, for example, to author's style, sense of humour, political beliefs, setting, or atmosphere. McFarlane provides the example of popular period films, which adapt contemporary works for their authors and readers but remote for their adapters and audience. Fidelity issues may be raised, for example, "to Dicken's London or to Jane Austen's village life", alongside their effect, since they risk "produc[ing] a distracting quaintness" (McFarlane 1996, p. 9). Fidelity criticism may be also adopted in light of McFarlane's approach towards transferable and non-transferable elements in adaptations. Not connected to the semiotic mode in which they appear, narrative elements may be simply and "faithfully" transferred from page to screen, whereas elements related to enunciation would be more subject to transformation (McFarlane 1996, p. 20). Accordingly and in simple terms, a successful adaptation would convey the same story themes, characters, plot, and capture the author's spirit, tone, style, while aspects including the temporal organisation or the setting may be transformed.

Intertextual Connections

As noted above, intertextuality holds a prominent position in the history of adaptation studies: for an extended period, critical research in adaptation has been closely related to that in intertextuality and the borders between the two areas have been blurred. Today, intertextuality as paradigm can still offer valid insights into the understanding of an adaptation. The conceptualisation of intertextuality is due to the French structuralist Genette (1997). Accordingly, the object of poetics is not the text considered in its singularity but rather "transtextuality", or "textual transcendence of text", that is "everything that connects a text, in a manifest or secret way, with other texts" (Genette 1997, p. 1). Transtextuality includes five different types of relations: intertextuality, paratextuality, metatextuality, hypertextualiy, and architextuality.

First, intertextuality was defined by Genette (1997, p. 2) as the actual presence of one text in another, with forms like citation, plagiarism, allusion, showing different degrees of acknowledgement. A less explicit and more distant relationship, paratextuality includes all that functions as a comment or frame for the actual body of the text, like title, subtitle, preface, postface, instructions, footnotes, images, cover (Genette 1997, p. 3). Third, metatextuality concerns the relation between two texts in which one critically comments on the other (Genette 1997, p. 4). Examples are literary or filmic critical rewritings, such as post-colonial or feminist rewritings of texts, which shade light on aspects that might have been omitted in the criticised work, or adopt a different viewpoint or contextualisation, or, again, feature a parody. Other examples are "unmarked adaptations" (Stam 2005, p. 30), which do not state their relation to an adapted text or literary genre but are actually influenced by them. Fourth, hypertextuality regards every relation which links a text, called hypertext, with a prior text, called hypotext. Hypertextual relations may derive from a process of transformation or from imitation (Genette 1997, p. 5). Last, architextuality is defined as the network of categories to which a single text belongs, including literary genres or discourse types (Genette 1997, p. 4), and can be described through terms like ballad, folk song, or TV series.

Hence, adaptations tackled in this work belong to Genette's fourth group of hypertextuality, encompassing textual transformation and transposition. In Hutcheon's terms (2013, p. XVI), adaptations are "deliberate, announced, and extended revisitations of prior works". The kind of textual derivation is made explicit through graded formulae such as "based on", "adapted from", "freely inspired from". Far from linear and smooth, such relations are, however, plural and multiverse, also because adaptations do not have only one precursor but a network of precursors (Elleström 2017; Leitch 2003; McFarlane 1996). Leitch argues (2003, p. 165) that: "adaptation study requires a sensitive and rigorous attention to the widest possible array of a film's precursor texts". For example, previous films by the adaptation director may offer intertextual clues for the understanding and appreciation of the artist's thematic or formal predilections or conventions. In turn, other adaptations of works of the same author may influence the viewer, by providing references, suggesting connections, pointing out some details. Again, an intertextual net may be activated by an actor of the film viewers have already seen in previous cinematographic narratives and who may influence the interpretation of the new film, due to the prior role or interpretation. The list of pathways is endless, and includes texts based on the same period, topic, setting, dialect, soundtrack, use of colour or of light. Connections may be extremely subjective and derive from background knowledge, as well as from personal interests. Multiple lines are not hierarchically ordered, as: "multiple versions exist laterally, not vertically" (Hutcheon 2013, p. XV). On these grounds, horizontal intertextuality excludes notions of authority and of authenticity underlying fidelity discourse.

Intertextuality as transtextual analysis implies addressing not only textual relations within the adapted story but also within the story of the adaptation. As such, the relation is not linear, as Elleström notices when mentioning "assisting media" like scores and libretti in adaption contexts (2017, p. 515). Leitch (2003), Stam (2005), and Elleström (2017) criticise the neglected history of assisting texts in adaptation criticism, as it challenges the adapted text-adaptation nexus in adaptation studies, as well as notions of authorship. In this vein, film adaptations of literary works technically imply an in-between stage of the screenplay, another "original" text that needs to be properly positioned and considered within the film's layered authorship. To make it more complex, screenplays may be written by the same director, by a different and specialised screenwriter, or by "a scripting committee" (McFarlane 1996, p. 35). We should ask, with Leitch (2003, p. 150), "[s]ince virtually all feature films work from a pre-existing written text, the screenplay, how is a film's relation to its literary source different from its relation to the screenplay?" The screenwriter's status and work need to cope with "the spectre of the novel's author, especially in the case of the classic or best-selling novel" and the "directorial signature" (McFarlane 1996, p. 35), if marked by celebrity status. In some cases, the author of the adapted text writes the screenwriter, works with the screenwriter as co-author or as consultant. Some may think that the author who knows the piece of literature is the best person who can write the script. By this, the author positions his screenwriter status as a guarantee of fidelity and authenticity of the film adaptation. However, the author is involved in a challenging process of re-writing his own text for a different medium, genre, and audience. On the one hand, this may be seen a process of questioning and challenging or, on the other hand, of controlling the film adaptation, to keep it closer to its author and to adapted text.

Adaptations, thus, raise and challenge issues of intertextuality both at the levels of codification and decodification. Understanding adaptations as adaptations means decoding the "palimpsestic

intertextuality" (Hutcheon 2013, p. 22) inherent in the transcodification, keeping the memory of the adapted texts while appreciating
the similarities and differences in the adaptation. Intertextuality,
thus, operates as a strategy for reading an adaptation, which may
differ from the intertextual horizon of the adapter. Hutcheon sustains (2013, p. 8) that adaptations should be regarded as enacting
"[a]n extended intertextual engagement with the adapted work".
This last concept needs further discussion.

Engaging Readers and Spectators

According to Hutcheon (2013), the very notion of intertextuality
lies at the crossroads of poetics and politics: it applies to texts, as
well as to people. If the aesthetic dimension has been discussed in
the previous section, the interpersonal perspective upon intertextuality is addressed here, with reference to interpersonal dynamics at stake in the processes of text codification and decodification.
Hutcheon (2013) identifies three main modes whereby audiences
engage with stories, namely the telling, showing, and interacting
modes. If the telling mode is based on the verbal semiotic system
for reading a novel, the showing mode implies the visual system
someone relies on when watching a film, whereas interaction occurs
when we use videogames. In such multifaceted situations, text re-
cipients become, in turn, readers, spectators, or players, and differently use their sensorial, emotional, and cognitive skills to decode
characters, settings, plots, themes, and motifs.

Clearly, all the telling, showing, and interacting modes of engagement are immersive, that is they involve audiences "imaginatively,
cognitively, and emotionally" (Hutcheon 2013, p. 23). Imagination
is at stake, for instance, when readers have to create their own personal image of a novel's characters, or when spectators have to imag-
ine the physical appearance of the character whose voice is audible
off-screen. Leitch (2003) denounces a widespread cliché whereby
books would stimulate imagination, whereas films would require a
reduced effort and offer ready images, pictures, and frames. This
is based, Leitch argues, on a fallaciously dichotomous assumption
the fact that "novels deal in concepts, films in percepts" (2003,
p. 156). Literary works would, accordingly, privilege the conceptual
and films would privilege the perceptual as a mode of experiencing
and appreciating the literary or film narrative. This simplistic distinction neglects, on the one hand, the multimodal configuration
and, on the other hand, the narrative unfolding of the filmic text.

More interestingly, cognitive engagement with adaptations depends on the presence of a knowing or an unknowing audience. In the case of familiarity with the adapted novel, the cognitive filter is inevitable, and the process of adaptation fruition unfolds through gap-filling with elements viewers retrieve from the adapted text (Hutcheon 2013, p. 121). Differently, the adaptation may also operate independently and make meaning without the prior knowledge of the literary text (McFarlane 1996, p. 21). Or, again, the adapted work may be consumed after the adaptation, thus subverting the predictable chronological order of fruition and turning the adaptation into the adapted text in the audience's experience. In this latest case, the previously mentioned personal image of the character cognitively shaped by the reader will be inevitably influenced by the image provided by the film.

Emotions play a pivotal role in adaptation fruition: audiences are emotionally attracted by adaptations as adaptations, but then emotionally dismiss adaptations as adaptations. Literature lovers want to watch a screen adaptation of a beloved work or of a work by a beloved author, but then condemn every deviation from the narrative they are familiar with as a form of betrayal. The pleasure of adaptation, Hutcheon sustains (2013, p. 114), "lies in their mixture of repetition and difference, of familiarity and novelty". Hence, adaptation offers the comfort of experiencing what is familiar, of knowing the story and its characters. If it were only this, however, it might "suggest the potentially conservative element in the audience response to adaptation" (Hutcheon 2013, p. 115). Yet, the real appeal of adaptations lies in the "simple act of almost but not quite repeating, in the revisiting of a theme with variations" (Hutcheon 2013, p. 115).

A cognitive and emotional phenomenon, engagement is also contextual, as the production and reception of the adaptation happen in a particular socio-cultural environment. McFarlane observes (1996, p. 21) that "conditions within the film industry and the prevailing cultural and social climate at the time of the film's making" are significant dynamics, especially when a time lapse exists in the time of the release. Change of place is also important in adaptation: new places of production and reception imply a new language, a new socio-cultural and artistic legacy, a new political system. Yet, issues of gender, ethnicity, religion, politics are particularly relevant in cross-cultural changes implied by the process of adaptation. Across transculturalisation, some tensions may be amplified, reduced, or redefined. On the one hand, a process of indigenisation may be enacted, whereby an intercultural encounter foregrounds dynamics of power and agency, against the backdrop of colonial and post-colonial discourses (Hutcheon 2013, p. 150). On the other hand, the transcultural phenomenon of Americanisation within a Hollywood context tends to blur national, regional, or historical specificities, in order to address and appeal international audiences (Hutcheon 2013, p. 147). Being engagement personal, social, and aesthetic, any definition of adaptation(s) needs to consider the multifold and multifaceted relations between different texts, between text and audience, and between text and context.

Adaptation as Process and as Product

The movement from fidelity to engagement in this introduction has progressively acknowledged the fact that the term "adaptation" is used "to refer to both a product and a process of creation and reception" (Hutcheon 2013, p. XV). A text transposition can be regarded either as a textual output regulated by genre constraints or as a process of codification and decodification, occurring in a given socio-cultural situation and involving different agents at various levels. As a matter of fact, these two approaches evoke the formal-cultural divide in adaptation studies detected by Elliott (2014), as well as Corrigan's complex perspective (2017).

By adopting frames and tools of disciplines including sociology, ethnography, anthropology, cultural studies, history, geography, and economics, process-focused adaptation analysis observes what happens around and about the adaptation, in the telling and re-telling of a story (Hutcheon 2013). Stories of adaptations involve historical, socio-cultural, economic factors behind the adaptation, as well as biographical information about the director(s). Hutcheon adopts a journalistic style in this kind of exploration, and raises issues related to who? why? where? when? what? how?

Questions pertaining to "who" involve the identity of the adapter, very often a plural and layered one, as previously suggested through the reference to the screenwriter's presence. Interestingly, the status of the adaptation author is formalised and regulated at a legal level, in the acquisition of the legal rights to adapt the work. The adapted work's author is, indeed, recognised the ownership of cultural and intellectual property. The legal, economic, and aesthetic authorship is then necessarily mentioned at all promotional stages, in trailers, posters, and advertisements. In turn, authorial acknowledgement is negotiated through the sociological filter of celebrity, which may regard the text author, the director, or the artists variously involved in the adaptation. We are more likely to accept "unfaithful" adaptations or clear "deviations" from the adapted text if the adaptation involves famous directors or actors. To the contrary, we tend to be more faithful to a faithful approach in case celebrity regards the adapted author.

Why-questions bring to the fore the range of motivations behind an adaptation (Stam 2005, p. 25). McFarlane observes (1996, p. 8) that adapters may conceive and choose a to-be-adapted text as "a source of ready-made material, in the crude sense of pre-tested stories and characters". Beyond merely financial exploitation, directors may decide to adapt a literary work to pay tribute, to celebrate, to promote, to comment, to criticise, to deconstruct, to contradict, to rewrite, only to provide some examples. While carrying out their primarily aesthetic, socio-cultural, or political project, they may express intimacy with or distance from the author and from the work. In turn, spectators may watch an adapted film because of their passion for the adapted work or for the director, out of simple curiosity, because they have been attracted by a marketing campaign or because they have been invited/advised by someone. All these motivations affect the decodification process emotionally and cognitively.

The extent to which the "where" and "when" adaptations are produced and consumed affects meaning-making has been discussed in the introduction. When stories travel across time and space, adaptations tend to transform. Not only because settings, historical backgrounds, political and cultural references may vary but also because sets of beliefs, sensitiveness, and awareness mutate. For instance, the time of writing is witnessing the so-called cancel-culture, which advocates the erasure of art forms, media products, academic events considered based on imbalance of power and offensive language. Originated in the USA, cancel culture later crossed national borders and is challenging processes of adaptation involving ethnic, gender, or economic inequalities.

By adopting qualitative and/or quantitative tools of literary, linguistic, stylistic analysis, or of translation studies, text-focused adaptation analysis is concerned with how a text adapts a previous text. A text-focused perspective regards narratological strategies of "selection, amplification, concretization, actualization, critique, extrapolation, popularization, reaccentuation, transculturalization" (Stam 2005, p. 45). Attention may be devoted to how the adaptation depicts the main character, the socio-political situation or, again, the geographical place operating as the setting for the narrative. In order to conduct this kind of research, analysts may look at specific registers or varieties of the verbal language, at the function of some semiotic resources like music, costume, or light. As a consequence, they may draw conclusions on how the text deals with the adapted story formally, functionally, and stylistically.

An interesting aspect in a text-based approach may be related to the generic configuration. The fact that short stories are chosen for the adaptation process explored in this volume may wrongly seem marginal. This is because traditional adaptation analysis had exclusively addressed the adaptation of novels, equalling literary texts with the novel, and simply obliterating short stories from any discussion and inspection. Elleström (2017, pp. 516, 517) observes that "it has always been taken for granted that short stories and plays may be source media for adaptation as well as novels". The effect of the "taking from granted" habit is that of genre invisibility. When discussing the widespread prejudice against adaptations in favour of adapted literary works, Leitch provocatively observes: "No critic to my knowledge has claimed that short stories are better than movies" (Leitch 2003, p. 155). This work, then, offers a contribution in critical gap-filling and includes short stories into the discussion on adaptations. My argument is that addressing the short-story adaptation enables us to deconstruct the novel-film dichotomy by questioning the very terms of the polarity.

Meanwhile, addressing short-story adaptation(s) provides interesting insights from the viewpoints of analysis and appreciation. Much criticism towards adaptations, indeed, condemns "how films 'reduce' great novels" (McFarlane 1996, p. 10). Alternative or complementary to the moral lens of adaptation evaluation, the quantitative criterion is equally dangerous, since it risks limiting the analysis to the listing of what has been "left out" from the adapted text. As a matter of fact, reduction and loss cannot be the analyst's criteria. The fact that the adapted text is inherently a short text implies that there is no need of quantitatively reducing the narrative in terms of events, actions, dialogue, and that attention can be given to the transcodification proper.

Hence, the adaptation analyst has to adopt a rigorous framework and toolkit, as advocated by numerous scholars in adaptation studies (Leitch 2003; McFarlane 1996). It seems to me that multimodal stylistic analysis is suitable to this multifold purpose. It is indeed a thorough and systemic frame, based on a network of formal parameters for making and understanding meaning in a text. Being focused on modes and modal resources for the shaping of style, it also offers insights into the peculiarity of the audio-visual texts addressed here. Since it is firmly grounded on the socio-semiotics of systemic functional linguistics, it is concerned with contextual dynamics affecting meaning-making in specific situations. This analytic framework seems to combine the inspection of adaptation as product and as process, as it involves text analysis in its formal and functional aspects, as well as of in its contextual dynamics. The illustration of this framework is the scope of the next chapter.

References

Bluestone, G. (1957) *Novel into Film: A Critical Study*, Baltimore, MD, The John Hopkins Press.

Cartmell, D., Whelehan, I. (1999) *Adaptation: From Text to Screen, Screen to Text*, London/New York, Routledge.

Cartmell, D. et al. (1996) *Pulping Fictions: Consuming Culture across the Literature/Media Divide*, Oxford, Blackwell.

Corrigan, T. (2017) Defining Adaptation, in T. Leitch (ed.) *The Oxford Handbook of Adaptation Studies*, Oxford, Oxford U.P., pp. 24–35.

Elleström, L. (2017) Adaptation and Intermediality, in T. Leitch (ed.) *The Oxford Handbook of Adaptation Studies*, op. cit., pp. 509–527.

Elleström, L. (2020) Transmediation: Some Theoretical Considerations, in N. Salmose, Elleström, L. (eds.) *Transmediations: Communications across Media Borders*, London/New York, Routledge, pp. 1–14.

Elliott, K. (2014) Formal-Cultural and Textual-Contextual Divides in Adaptation Studies, *Literature/Film Quarterly*, 42:4, pp. 576–593.

Genette, G. (1997) *Palimpsests: Literature in the Second Degree*. Channa Newman and Claude Doubinski, trans., Lincoln, University of Nebraska Press.

Hutcheon, L. with O'Flynn, S. (2013 [2006]) *A Theory of Adaptation*, 2nd ed., London/New York, Routledge.

Jellenik, G. (2017) On the Origins of Adaptation, as Such: The Birth of a Simple Abstraction, in T. Leitch (ed.) *The Oxford Handbook of Adaptation Studies*, op. cit., pp. 37–52.

Leitch, T. (2003) Twelve Fallacies in Contemporary Adaptation Theory, *Criticism*, 45:2, pp. 149–171.

Leitch, T.M. (ed.) (2017) *The Oxford Handbook of Adaptation Studies*, op. cit.

McFarlane, B. (1996) *Novel to Film: An Introduction to the Theory of Adaptation*, Oxford, Clarendon Press.

Stam, R. (2005) Introduction: The Theory and Practice of Adaptation, in R. Stam, A. Raengo (eds.) *Literature and Film: A Guide to the Theory and Practice of Film Adaptation*, Oxford, Blackwell, pp. 1–52.

Woolf, V. (1926) The Cinema, *The Nation and Athenaeum*, July 6.

2 Multimodal Stylistic Analysis

Multimodal Stylistics

Stylistics is generally considered to descend from the classic art of rhetoric, more specifically, *elocutio*, the art of selecting the appropriate style for a desired effect. As an approach within the field of applied linguistics, stylistics aims to provide an accurate and detailed analysis of texts using the tools of linguistics (Toolan 2014, p. 455). Sometimes called "literary linguistics", stylistics traditionally investigated literary texts but nowadays increasingly addresses a broader range of academic, medical, and journalistic texts (Burke 2014, p. 1). Stylistics also encompasses various models such as formalism and functionalism, which tackle different types of issues. If formalism is concerned with formal patterns and structures, functionalism invites an examination of the functional components of language and style.

As a layered approach, stylistics includes a variety of established sub-fields which address specific domains, issues, and aims and rely on distinct tools and toolkits. For example, while pedagogical stylistics is concerned with education, translation stylistics explores interlinguistic transfer. Other sub-fields are feminist stylistics, focused on denouncing and subverting sexist language, and corpus stylistics that relies on computer-based support in the compilation of text corpora for stylistic enquiries. Of particular interest to this volume, multimodal stylistics is one of the most flourishing sub-fields in stylistics (Burke 2014; Nørgaard 2014).

Developed across the last two decades (McIntyre 2008), the framework of multimodal stylistic analysis integrates stylistics and multimodality. As Linda Pillière explains, "[m]ultimodal stylistics […] aims to use literary stylistics with multimodal theory to analyse texts". She clarifies (2014, p. 100) that: "the role of multimodal stylistics is to demonstrate how the different semiotic resources

DOI: 10.4324/9781003183846-3

interact to produce meaning". To this aim, multimodal stylistic analysis explores stylistic systems that go beyond the verbal, a range of distinct and alternative modes such as costume and gesture that often co-occur with language in its written or oral forms. Within the multimodal ensemble, modes are conceived as resources for making meaning and for shaping style (Kress and van Leeuwen 2001, 2006).

Multimodal stylistics has devoted most attention to space and time-based texts, which involve either simultaneous or sequential meaning-making. On the one hand, analysis of static texts considers the choice, combination, and organisation of graphic features such as typography, imagery, or blank spaces. An example is Nørgaard's inspection of the semiotics of paper and the materiality of the novel (2014, p. 478). On the other hand, analysis of dynamic textuality is explored in films, TV series, and YouTube videos. In his study of Loncraine's 1995 film adaptation of Shakespeare's *Richard III*, McIntyre argued (2008, p. 327) that

> a stylistic analysis of film may lead to a greater understanding of the principles behind the adaptation of plays, novels and short stories into films, and may lead us to be able to speculate on, for example, why adaptations sometimes restructure the order of events in the original narrative, or why certain elements of plot are left out.

In multimodal stylistics, Nørgaard (2014, p. 471) identifies two main approaches: a cognitive one, concerned with the psychological effects of multimodal literature, and a socio-semiotic one that aims to develop descriptive grammars for all the semiotic modes in terms of contextual meaning-making. The socio-semiotic approach is grounded in Kress and van Leeuwen's (2001) four-strata model of communication:

- discourse (socially constructed knowledges of some aspect of the world);
- design (choice of mode, as semiotic resources for realising discourse and interaction);
- production (choice of medium, intended for the material support of communication);
- distribution (related to modes and forms of reaching the audience).

The signifying system of a film is, accordingly, read in light of the themes, issues, and beliefs it tackles, its modal and medial components, as well as its role in informing and being informed by the context(s) of distribution and fruition. As such, the socio-semiotic approach fits into the theoretical conceptualisation outlined in the previous chapter, which suggests that an adaptation should be considered as both product and process, as a site where formal, functional, and contextual dynamics intertwine.

A Socio-Semiotic Metafunctional Framework

The socio-semiotic approach proposed here adopts the metafunctional framework outlined by Halliday (1978) and Halliday and Hasan (1985). Conceived as strands of meaning, the three Hallidayan metafunctions encompass the predominant purposes of language:

- the ideational metafunction, concerned with the expression of content (human, natural, and cultural environments);
- the interpersonal metafunction, focused on social relations among interactive participants (speakers/listeners, authors/readers, directors/spectators);
- the textual metafunction, involved in the construction of the text (organisation, cohesion and coherence).

The metafunctional value of film texts is analysed within their compositional units: frames, shots, scenes, and sequences (Bordwell 1991; Bordwell and Thompson 2012). The first consists in a still, or static shot, while the second is an unedited film unit, a continuous and uninterrupted take. Composed of a number of interrelated shots, a scene is a single time–space unit, while sequences are larger diegetic units, including introductions or conclusions. Among these levels, the shot is generally taken by film text analysts as the basic meaningful video unit (Bordwell 1991; Bordwell and Thompson 2012), with its role and function corresponding to those of the clause in linguistics. Within the shot, the staging of an action and the way it is shot by the camera in terms of e.g., scale, distance, and lighting, constitute the *mise en scène,* thus showing an internal organisation (Giannetti 1993, p. 486). Shots and scenes are also sequentially and logically organised through the syntactic process of editing or montage. In the multimodal filmic artefact, in other terms, the three metafunctions are temporally realised and integrated: a range of co-occurring modes and modal resources composing the visual and audio tracks unfold over time and across shots, scenes, and sequences.

The visual track that audiences see on screen encompasses dynamic images of participants and their actions. Participants include the human, natural, and cultural elements of the *mise en scène*. These elements make gestures and movements or perform actions in the setting in which they are immersed, which itself can be static (e.g., a restaurant) or dynamic (e.g., a moving car). Change and movement in a given setting can also be related to natural phenomena such as snowfall or rainfall, which exhibit different durations, speeds, and rhythms. Any setting, in turn, can be natural or artificial and enjoy various types of relationships to the participants, for example, as the site where people live, work, think, move, or relax. The specific positions actors and objects occupy and their reciprocal relations within the *mise en scène* can suggest their modes and forms of interaction, as well as their degrees of relevance to an action or to the viewer.

Unlikely to be objectively represented, participants and actions are captured from a specific perspective and distance. Angles and size of frame may establish diverse subjective dynamics of perception, which then vary when the camera moves along different trajectories, with variable durations and effects (Bordwell 1991; Bordwell and Thompson 2012). Sometimes spectators are offered the viewpoint of a character, in a point-of-view shot (PoV shot) that may reveal what that character sees and from the position s/he occupies. Subjectivity may also project feelings, dreams, and memories and be expressed through colour and light choices, changes, and contrasts (Branigan 1984, p. 6).

The audio track can be explored by what van Leeuwen (1999) calls the "soundscape", a composition of voice, music, and sound effects, these last of which can have either a natural (e.g., the sound of rain) or artificial nature (e.g., a car horn). In every situation, different natural and/or artificial sounds coexist and interact (e.g., a doorbell interrupting human chats in a room), originating from different sources and propagating in different directions, with different degrees of intensity and relevance to listeners. The soundscape unfolds in time, being a dynamic and fluid entity where sounds change over time in terms of their presence, absence, intensity, and interactions, either naturally or, in the case of film, as a result of will and/or manipulation (e.g., volume increase and decrease in film music). Non-speech sounds may, then, be classified as diegetic or extra-diegetic: the former includes sounds that naturally form part of the story space, the latter encompasses sounds that are added during the editing process (Toolan 2014, p. 456). If we hear a piece of music produced during a piano concert shown on screen, we have diegetic music; if the same music accompanies a dinner-party scene and has been added at the post-production stage, it is considered non-diegetic.

A filmic soundscape is also aurally perceived and its meaning is affected by modes and forms of perception (Branigan 1984, p. 96). First, by the hearing position, which may conflate with that of a character (aural PoV or point of hearing). Second, by the hearing extent, which may be restricted and limited to that of a specific character. Third, by the hearing quality, which may be temporarily or permanently impaired or enhanced by natural, artificial, or physiological factors (Branigan 1984, p. 94). Generally, sound may be or appear to be neutral or may be a projection of character. In subjective scenes, it may be remembered, dreamed, or imagined (Branigan 1984, p. 97). Within the film soundscape, especially in adaptation studies, spoken discourse is of utmost importance and will be addressed in the following section.

Forms and Functions of Speech

The analysis of speech in adaptations of literary works showcases a paradox. On the one hand, it has been traditionally dismissed by film theorists, including Eisenstein, Pudovkin, Arnheim, Rotha, and Kracauer (Kozloff 2000, p. 62), who celebrated the primarily visual nature of film. On the other hand, it is welcomed by adaptation scholars, since it provides the semiotic system that most simply and smoothly "transfers" the literary text to the screen, for example, through dialogue or voice-over (Hutcheon 2013). If the former overlooked the inherently multimodal configuration of film, the latter neglected the fact that within the adapted filmic artefact, speech is far from a mere translation of the page. First, because of the transformative process inherent in the adaptation process discussed in the previous chapter. Second, because of the multiple authors of speech, including "casting directors, actors, directors, cameramen, editors, composers, sound recordists, mixers, and editors" (Kozloff 2000, p. 122). At every stage, these professionals are responsible for the changes that occur from the printed script to the spoken text actualised within the multimodal film: "words in a script become transfigured when they are spoken by an actor, filmed by the camera, edited together, underscored with music" (Kozloff 2000, p. 90).

A multimodal stylistic approach seems to acknowledge this tension, by addressing both speech content and form within a multimodal ensemble, as transformed by the process of adaptation. In this way, filmic speech is accorded attention for the specific ways in which it engages with the adapted text in terms of: what linguistic elements of the text are adopted; how these elements are altered from a syntactic and pragmatic perspective; and where they are used in the film. Alongside content analysis, for instance, human voice is critically described in terms of gender and age, as well as in terms of voice quality (van Leeuwen 1999). At the same time, voice is socio-culturally and psychologically meaningful; it reflects social or ethnic group membership, as well as the psychological and/or emotional profile of speakers (Kozloff 2000). Hence, voice type and quality are not random choices within film meaning-making: film-makers strive to find exactly the right voice quality, accent, and inflections for their subject matter (Kozloff 2000, p. 75). Actors, moreover, modulate their voices in order to express relaxed, sentimental, ironic, or authoritative tones (Kozloff 1988, p. 95). Notably then, filmic voice can be described by the position it occupies on- and off-screen: in the first case, it is generally used in dialogues among characters; in the second case, it mainly expresses the narrator's voice. In the following sections, I rely extensively on Kozloff's studies of film dialogue (2000) and voice-over (1988).

Film Dialogues and the Voice-In

Dialogue, Kozloff argues (2000, p. 28), is the most neglected area in cinema studies, conceptualised in a simplistic manner and addressed in a superficial and prescriptive way. In turn, screenwriting manuals recommend keeping dialogue to a minimum and avoiding obscure, flowery, repetitive speech. In film adaptations, however, dialogue holds a distinct role, as it is likely to evoke the adapted text; therefore, it greatly contributes to a film's appeal and value. Meanwhile, it may challenge screenwriters, who hesitate between dialogue transposition from page to screen and more active engagement.

Kozloff (2000) proposes an analytical approach to film dialogue, involving a number of formal parameters. The first criterion quantifies the presence and quantity of film dialogue, detecting scenes with and without speech (speechless scenes) and the presence of long stretches of speech within speech scenes (long turns). The use and extent of dialogue interact with scene content, for instance, "montage sequences compressing time, chase scenes, dances, and lovemaking are particularly likely to be presented with no speech whatsoever" (Kozloff 2000, p. 65). Speechless scenes are generally accompanied by diegetic or non-diegetic sound effects or music. Cinematographic long turns to the opposite "allow for the explanation of a complicated argument or the description of a past narrative event. They contribute greatly to character revelation. They keep our attention focused on a star performance" (Kozloff 2000, p. 67). This is the case of frequent long turns in *Adaptation* (2002) by Spike Jonze, with Nicholas Cage expressing the challenges of writing a script. The fractured and disconnected interior monologues configure a space of tension between voice-in and voice-off: Cage is on screen but is not actually speaking.

The second parameter is the number of participants in a conversation: film dialogue may feature a monologue, a dialogue, or a polylogue. In monologues, Kozloff argues (2000, p. 70), speakers talk to animals, mirrors, the dead, to themselves. In dialogues and polylogues, modes and forms of conversational interaction are of interest, with particular attention paid to turn-taking, which may unfold sequentially, with pauses of different duration, or simultaneously, through interruptions or overlapping (van Leeuwen 1999, p. 71).

Kozloff (2000, p. 33) identifies two groups of functions served by film dialogues: the first relates mostly to content and the second to style. As for the former, dialogues may play a role in defining place and time, in providing information related to past events, in communicating narrative causality and enacting narrative events, as well as in naming characters. As such, dialogues can also perform characterisation through dialects, accents, vocal qualities, and skills. The latter stylistic function may be more related to stylistic effects or to ideological dynamics, such as poetic effects, jokes, and humour or the expression of political, religious, and moral viewpoints. Consequently, dialogue may draw the viewer's attention to something so as to control mood, emotions, and interpretations.

Far from remaining discrete, these functions can operate simultaneously in film dialogues, especially in the case of adaptations of literary works. They are also enriched through alternations or co-occurring verbal strategies such as intertitles or voice-over, a topic that is addressed in the following paragraphs. More broadly, film dialogue interacts with other audio-visual modes. In Kozloff's words (2000, p. 14), "[m]any of the ways in which narrative is communicated, empathy elicited, themes conveyed, visuals interpreted come from the interaction of the words with the visual images". Not all modes integrate with dialogue to the same degree; the most proximate are, according to Kozloff (2000, p. 93): "performance, shot content and scale, editing, and sound design". Specifically, vocal performance depends on pace, that is speed, pause and rhythm, as well as on intonation (i.e., the rise and fall of pitch during the spoken utterance). Volume plays a role in vocal performance, indicating whether words are uttered softly or loudly. These parameters convey emotions and are often accompanied by gestures. Shot content and scale also make meaning in interplay with dialogue, as this chapter will discuss in a later section.

Screen/Story Boundaries and the Voice-Over

In her monographic study on American fiction film, Kozloff (1988, p. 5) defines the voice-over narration as: "oral statements, conveying any portion of a narrative, spoken by an unseen speaker situated in a space and time other than that simultaneously being presented by the images on the screen". This definition foregrounds the auditory dimension and the variable extent of the voice-over unit, as well as its intersemiotic configuration: it can only be identified through the relation between the auditory presence of the voice and the visual absence of the speaker. It then refers to the gap it generates between the space and time of the utterance and the space and time of the narrative. Ultimately, it draws attention to the placement, frequency, and duration of the voice-over unit across the film: generally intermittent, the voice-over can be minimally or extensively heard across the text.

The voice-over may belong to a narrator (mainly addressed by Kozloff in her study) or to a character. In the first case, it may encode a frame narrator who tells the story from some spatial-temporal position outside of the story boundaries (Kozloff 1988, p. 50). Often heterodiegetic, the frame narrator remains invisible throughout the text: taking a privileged vantage point, s/he may adopt the role of a voice-of-God storyteller and convey an authoritative, nostalgic, or more detached tone. Among the most common ideational tasks of the voice-over frame narrator is that of introducing the characters and the plot and of defining the time and place of the narrative events. S/he can precisely locate the story by a simple phrase, explain and/or compress story events, or flash forward and backward in time, that is, activate narrative leaps from the present to the past or future (Gordejuela 2019, p. 125). The voice-over frame narrator can thus indicate synchronicity between the current discourse and story or alternatively signal temporal distance, comparing and contrasting historical ages and moments. From a textual viewpoint, s/he knits together all narrative threads (Kozloff 1988, p. 80).

Closer to the voice-in, a less distant voice-over can represent the focaliser rather the narrator. Unlike the exterior "frame narrator", the "embedded narrator" corresponds to Genette's homodiegetic narrator, who participates in the action. This stance is defined by Kozloff as the "character-narrator", and s/he may be manifested through an interior monologue voice-over offering us more intimate knowledge of the characters, by revealing their individuality and subjectivity of perception and storytelling. In this case, the speaker is on screen but is not talking. If frame narrators in adaptations often speak in conjunction with shots of pages from their novels, embedded narrators often present their stories as memoirs, diaries, or letters (Kozloff 1988, p. 52). With a hybrid solution, an on-scene character and audible voice-over may be used to disconnect the narrated self in the past from the narrating self in the present. An intersemiotic clash may be generated between, for example, a mature voice and a young actor representing the same character. Sometimes a camera off may be used; when "the speaker is merely temporarily off-camera, the camera could pan around the same scene and capture the speaker" (Kozloff 1988, p. 3). Not necessarily a unique stance, different voice-over speakers can engage with and impact the film narrative in various ways.

In filmic discourse, the voice-over technique plays an important interpersonal role. Indeed, the voice-over narrator is always speaking to someone (e.g., the theatre audience or cinema spectators), and his/her storytelling shapes the filmic story as a deliberate and conscious communicative act (Kozloff 1988, p. 51). On the one hand, the voice-over "creates a special relationship with the viewer", "a feeling of connection and intimacy" (Kozloff 1988, p. 129). On the other hand, it guides and orients the spectators in their interpretations and conclusions, in shaping their ideological and moral positions about the film (Kozloff 1988, p. 80). From a textual viewpoint, voice-overs offer "prominent composition devices" (Harrison 2020, p. 22), serving as more than smooth transitions between scenes, as

Forceville points out (2002, p. 130) in his analysis of the screen adaptation of a novel by McEwan, *The Comfort of Strangers*.

Clearly, voice-over narration occurs simultaneously with moving images, which rely on the position and movements of the camera, lighting, scenery, properties, dialogue, and music (Kozloff 1988, p. 102). Different effects can be achieved through a range of audio-visual intersemiotic configurations, including overlapping, complementarity, or contradiction (Kozloff 1988, p. 102). For example, in her multimodal inspection of the first TV series of *The Handmaid's Tale*, Harrison (2020, p. 36) notes that the voice-over, combined with visual strategies, has the effect of distancing June/Offred from her own tale, shaping a "split self" that makes the speaker more a witness than an experiencer. Elsewhere, dissonant effects are often achieved through the interplay with music.

Lyrics, Volume, Melodies

Ingham foregrounds (2017, p. 324) that the song form is an intrinsically "adaptive" genre, as it undergoes important variation across ages, cultures, domains, and genres. The fact that a song may be chosen as a film soundtrack seems to instantiate a further process of mutation. As a matter of fact, Ingham distinguishes between intra-medial and intermedial adaptation. The song may first experience intramedial "transformations, variations, transcriptions, trans-positions, restylings" (Ingham 2017, p. 325), for instance, through covers by other singers, tribute groups, performers, or reinterpretations by the same artist. Or it may be intermedially recontextual-ised within another art form, such as a video game, ballet, opera, or theatre performance. In the new situation, music inhabits a new medial form, where it co-occurs with other and different modes. This happens as a result of a process of adaptation, which acquires poignancy within the process examined in this volume. While existing music may be chosen to accompany the screen images, film music may be specifically composed for a film or TV series and is then called a score. Testifying to the crucial function music plays in filmic semiosis, the music composer is acknowledged as one of the film's authors (Hutcheon 2013, p. 312).

The effects of film music can unfold on a conscious or sub-conscious level, but, according to Kalinak (2010), are strongest when they happen below the threshold of viewer awareness. Meaning-making is also related to the multimodal configuration of the soundtrack, that is, to the presence of lyrics and melody, of words and music (Inglis 2012; Kalinak 2010). If the music has lyrics, it performs a largely ideational metafunction, suggesting events and actions or specifying time and place. Alternatively, it may act at the level of characterisation, revealing characters' thoughts, feelings, emotions, interests, and motivations. It may carry socio-cultural meanings, as when traditional popular songs shape the cultural context of a film or politically symbolic songs mark the political valence of a film. In the case of an adaptation, a piece of music may express continuity or discontinuity, by confirming or changing the thematic, political, or socio-cultural perspective outlined by the adapted text.

By contrast, instrumental music mainly operates at the interpersonal level and can easily create an atmosphere or mood, so that the audience reacts to what they are watching. This emotional impact is especially true when a famous piece of music is used: a recognisable song can evoke powerful emotions and encourage the audience to establish an emotional connection to the film or TV series they are watching. Music can also emphasise suspense, control emotional shift, and offer a warning to audiences to be prepared for a significant action (Giannetti 1993, p. 198ff).

Music can also act at a textual level, both within and across shots. Musical changes can be effective strategies to mark crucial emotional moments or suggest narrative developments. Volume variation can underscore speech: many dialogue scenes play out with no music or with an almost imperceptible low background score so that the audience can better hear the words (Kozloff 2000, p. 118). Volume variation can then be used to reinforce or foreshadow elements on- and off-screen. Like music, sound effects are usually subordinated to dialogue: "used unobtrusively underneath speech to create naturalistic noises such as footsteps, door openings, and dish rattling, or to enhance the realism of off-screen space through traffic sounds, dogs barking, or crowd noise" (Kozloff 2000, p. 119). Sounds can also operate in a similar way to voiceovers by connecting images that might seem disconnected and sustaining structural unity across the whole film narrative. This may be the case with transitional devices such as the sound bridge: "whereby the sound over a shot comes from the space of a previous shot" (Berthin-Scaillet 2010, p. 160). In this editing technique, meaning is projected through tension between the discontinuity of visual transitions and the continuity expressed through sound.

Words on the Screen

Sometimes language is instantiated in film discourse as writing, and this occurs either in the form of inserts or intertitles. The former includes verbal texts within the diegesis such as signs, newspaper articles, and letters. The latter include writing, either on a blank screen or superimposed over the dynamic image of the film. Intertitles make additional meaning through the use of writing styles (font type, face, size, colour) in relation to the background (background colour, layout, style if neutral or the image it is superimposed on).

Overall, intertitles are used to provide film audiences with necessary narrative information (Kozloff 1998, p. 24) about time, space, characters, and historical background and can be considered as the ancestors to voice-over narration. After sound tracks became an established element in film, dialogues and/or voice-overs replaced intertitles in many but not all of their functions (Robinson 2012, p. 33). In spite of detractions by purists who favour visual-only film, their continuing relevance is demonstrated by the fact that they survived long after the era of the silent film and are still adopted in contemporary films.

If their main function is ideational, intertitles can also serve interpersonal functions, by establishing a particular atmosphere, tone, or flavour. They can also be adopted to create connections and/or disconnections among sequences within the film narrative, thus operating at the level of cohesion and sustaining comprehension of the text. Robinson argues (2012, p. 33) that intertitles engage audiences differently, by demanding they read rather than merely watch a film. This shift draws attention to the multimodal configuration of the filmic artefact and to the multisensorial engagement it requires. It also foregrounds the relevance of apparently minor items within the film meaning-making system and, more specifically, within the adaptation process.

Size of Frame and Angles

The visual parameter of size of frame is central to the presentation and depiction of human, natural and cultural participants. Technically, the codification of size of frame refers to the specific sections of the human body depicted in an image: while close-ups capture the character's head and shoulders, medium shots show human bodies from the knees up, and long shots display full figures. As a matter of fact, the semiotic system can also be applied to the repre-sentation of objects, whereby only a detail, a portion, or the whole item can be depicted. Unlike the static and frozen size of frame realised by a photograph, size of frame is a fluid and systemic fea-ture within the filmic narrative. It may be achieved through camera movement, for instance, using a progressive or regressive camera movement or a zooming process. Or it may result from editing and follow a transition, generally a cut, in a dialogue scene of a subjec-tive shot. In ideational terms, the long shot enables to capture a character's movements and actions, while the close-up may suggest introspection, access to the character's thoughts, memories, feel-ings, and emotions (Hutcheon 2013, p. 59).

The main effect of the enactment of size of frame is establishing social distance between the characters and the audience: close shots shape an intimate distance, medium shots a personal distance, and long shots an impersonal distance (Kress and van Leeuwen 2006, p. 124). As a matter of fact, the represented participant can be touched at close personal distance, while public distance suggests an imper-sonal relationship and depicts interactive participants as strangers. Social distance is thus a graded parameter, developing on a cline of intimacy that ranges from close to far personal distance, to public social distance. The analysis of social distance is key for the under-standing of characterisation and setting, both independently and in their mutual relations.

In the film narrative, the process of framing interpersonal re-lations with an audience is also achieved through perspective, that is the adoption of specific angles. If size of frame expresses social distance among participants, angles establish relations of power (Kress and van Leeuwen 2006, p. 129). Like size of frame, perspective is a graded system, although three main angles can be identified. A high angle gives interactive participants power over represented ones; a low angle gives represented participants power over interactive ones; eye level indicates equality in an established power relation. The depiction of angles can be articulated at the syntagmatic level through editing devices or can be inscribed within a dynamic process related to camera movement.

Movements

Motion within a shot can relate to a represented participant (a hu-man being running, moving train, falling rain) or to the camera itself. For example, participants can perform lateral movements on the screen and specific movements have certain meanings: an upward motion tends to suggest "aspiration, joy, power, and authority", whereas a downward movement tends to suggest "grief, death, insignificance, depression, weakness" (Giannetti 1993, p. 82). Movement to the right conveys natural feelings and projects the values of determination and efficiency, while movement to the left seems "tense and uncomfortable" (Giannetti 1993, p. 82). Alternatively, participants may perform depth movements, by moving towards or away from the camera. The effect of a depth movement depends on the kind of character who performs it: an attractive character moving towards the camera (and thus towards the audience) may look friendly, a negative character moving towards the camera may seem menacing. In general, motion towards the camera depicts an assertive and confident character (Giannetti 1993, p. 82).

On-screen movement can be produced by either a static or moving camera. Conveying a sense of stability and order (Giannetti 1993, p. 101), a static camera may be mounted on a tripod and, from that position, then moved either along the horizontal axis (panning) or the vertical axis (tilting) or, again, moving towards an object or person (zooming). A panning shot may be used to show the vastness of a natural landscape, or to express the connections between people in a given situation. The tilt often constructs a low angle and highlights the vertical orientation of a tree or a tower or traces the vertical trajectory in a PoV shot, with the camera tilting downwards or upwards (Giannetti 1993, p. 98). A zoom may be used to foreground a detail in a room or on a face, and operate as a trigger for a flashback sequence.

Alternatively, the camera can be mounted on a moving vehicle like a car, as a dolly. Used for more dynamic effects, the dolly can move in, out, alongside a moving item. Overall, slow tracking a character may suggest gradual psychological revelation (Giannetti 1993, p. 100ff) or signal relevance. If a hand-held camera is used, movements lose their smoothness; they are exaggerated and acquire a blurred effect that communicates instability and uncertainty. Crane shots are airborne dolly shots: cranes lift the camera in or out of a scene and can move up, down, diagonally, in, out, or any combination of these. Not only do movement directionality and smoothness make meaning; speed-related techniques such as slow or fast motion affect narrative rhythm, as they decrease or increase the pace of unfolding actions and events. If slow motion can ritualise, solemnise the scene, suggest speculation, or indicate flashbacks (Giannetti 1993, p. 113), fast motion can intensify natural speed or create comic effects in the case of acceleration (Giannetti 1993, p. 112).

Colour and Light Choices and Changes

Chromatic choices, contrasts, and changes realise ideational, inter-personal, and textual functions, both at the levels of *mise en scène* and editing. Considered as hues, colours can be used to denote or describe people, places, and objects, like in flags or brands. How-ever, tints tend to be primarily emotional in their appeal and suggest moods and feelings more than objects. They may be associated with adjectives in linguistics, and with melodies in music. In general, cool colours tend to project tranquillity, aloofness, and serenity, whereas warm colours tend to suggest aggressiveness, violence, and stimulation (Giannetti 1993, pp. 20, 21). In this interpersonal role, they may be considered in their degrees of saturation or modula-tion, namely in their vividness and vibrancy or in their shaded and blurred nature (van Leeuwen 2011). Pale or intense grades of the same tint may express different feelings and moods, and the same is valid for its flat or modulated versions. Finally, colours may ful-fil compositional functions and operate in terms of indicating dis/continuity within the film narrative or between the adapted text and the adaptation. As such, colour differentiation may be of in-terest. Differentiation can be measured on a scale that goes from a wide and varied palette of colours, through a reduced palette, to monochrome. This parameter may affect both the *mise en scène* for colour combination within the scene, and editing as for colour changes across the scenes. Rather than a binary and dichotomic system, based on the opposition of abstract and absolute colours, colour is indeed a parametric, graded system (van Leeuwen 2011), and, in the filmic narrative, it is used as a fluid and dynamic semi-otic and aesthetic resource (Giannetti 1993).

The semiotic system of colour is interconnected to that of light. In their grammar of visual design, Kress and van Leeuwen (2006, p. 152) identify two light-related markers: illumination, concerned with light sources, and brightness, related to light intensity. Light may be natural or artificial. Natural light may be given by the sun at sunrise, midday, or sunset and may be warm or cold. Artificial light may be generated by a lamp, a fire, or fireworks, creating a range of effects, also in relation to the numerous symbolic conno-tations that light conveys. Both natural and artificial light can take on varying degrees of intensity: low, soft, intense, vibrant, or vivid.

Low and cold light may be adopted to express intimacy, romanticism, sublimity, whereas intense and warm light generally projects values of socialisation, fun, and hospitality. Moreover, light directionality is used to highlight and make items salient, by generating lighting contrasts between a lit foregrounded element and the darker background. A director may guide the viewer's gaze towards a specific area of the scene through highly selective spotlights. This kind of lighting can evoke threats or romantic feelings or produce ethereal or sinister effects. Different styles of lighting are required for specific themes, moods, and genres. Tragedies tend to be represented using high contrasts (lights and darks), comedies in an overall high key (bright lighting), mysteries in a low key (diffused shadows) (Giannetti 1993, pp. 14–18). In this vein, light may be used in a realistic or expressionistic way, not only for description but also for characterisation. Giannetti (1993, p. 22) offers the example of the gangsters in the *Godfather* who are depicted through darkness and shadows. All the parameters of illumination, brightness, directionality, and effect are used at the level of the *mise en scène* and at the level of montage, through light continuity, change, or contrast across scenes and sequences.

If here addressed and illustrated independently, modes and modal resources like light or music can only be understood in their meaning-making when explored via their interactions. In a cinematographic narrative, the visual and audio tracks are interconnected and this interplay generates a range of implicatures and additional meaning. Audio and visual systems co-occur and integrate at various levels, degrees, and with both consonant and dissonant effects. If intersemiotic consonance is rather unproblematic for text fruition, dissonant relations between audio and visual tracks may be used to convey psychological and emotional intensity or tension, as well as to anticipate diegetic twists. Intersemiotic relations significantly affect editing and its semiotic value.

Beyond the Shot

Film units are joined and structured into an edited sequence, through editing or montage (Giannetti 1993, p. 118ff). Such syntactic organisation establishes logical, temporal, and diegetic relations among film basic units, including action fragmentation, PoV shifts, associations and contrasts among characters, situations, and events. Since the duration of an event and the duration of a shot are not equal, editing enables condensing or expanding actions and time on the screen. Editing compresses time, for example, through cuts or fast motion. Other connecting ties are fades-in, fades-out, and time-lapse dissolves, which visually render those verbal temporal transitions like "and", "meanwhile", "before", and "after". Transition ties shape rhythm in the cinematographic narrative, with cuts suggesting speed and fades slowing down the rhythm. They can also disrupt temporal continuity via analeptic and proleptic movements, as well as temporal ellipsis (Hutcheon 2013, p. 63ff).

As an alternative to the sequential juxtaposition of shots, the film may use parallel editing, alternating shots from one scene with shots from another taken in a different location. Alternations can be repeated through cross-cutting, to develop a specific theme or to suggest comparisons. Alternatively, scene combinations can be used to establish a shot-reverse-shot structure, for example, in a dialogue scene, where one speaker can be seen from the point of view of the other, and then the next speaker can be seen from the perspective of the first one. Editing also helps to establish a PoV shot, whereby the camera assumes the spatial position and viewpoint of a specific character. In PoV shots, spectators will see what the character sees, in terms of framing, dynamism, duration, and sharpness (Branigan 1984). The subjective PoV is not only visual, as it may be further and intersemiotically constructed through integration with sound effects such as music or voice-over narratives. Hence, filmic continuity achieved through editing can be primarily physical, if dominated by actions and events; psychological, if predominantly involved with subjective perception; or thematic, when it develops a motif or theme.

This chapter has illustrated multimodal stylistics as a sub-field of stylistics concerned with the coexistence and integration of modes and modal resources in a semiotic artefact. Adopting a socio-semiotic metafunctional framework enables us to raise formal and cultural issues about both the adaptation process and the adaptation text. Given the impossibility of a complete presentation of cinematographic meaning-making systems, the chapter has considered a selection of modes within the metafunctional framework. Modalities of particular relevance for the adaptation of literary works have been focused on, which relate to the transfer from a language-based to an audio-visual medium (e.g., voice-over and voice-in), as well as semiotic specificity in filmic discourse (e.g., camera movement and music).

References

Berthin-Scaillet, A. (2010) A Reading of *Away from Her,* Sarah Polley's Adaptation of Alice Munro's Short Story *The Bear Came Over the Mountain, The Journal of the Short Story in English,* 55, pp. 157–171.

Bordwell, D. (1991) *Making Meaning: Inference and Rhetoric in the Interpretation of Cinema,* Cambridge MA, Harvard U.P.

Bordwell, D., Thompson, K. (2012) *Film Art: An Introduction,* 10th ed., New York, McGraw Hill.

Branigan, E. (1984) *Point of View in the Cinema: A Theory of Narration and Subjectivity in Classical Film,* Berlin, Mouton.

Burke, M. (ed.) (2014) *The Routledge Handbook to Stylistics,* London/New York, Routledge.

Forceville, C. (2002) The Conspiracy in The Comfort of Strangers: Narration in the Novel and in the Film, *Language and Literature,* 11:2, pp. 119–135.

Giannetti, L. (1993) *Understanding Movies,* Boston, MA, Pearson.

Gordejuela, A. (2019) Understanding Retrospection: Blended Joint Attention and Multimodal Construction of Film Flashbacks, *Language and Literature,* 28:2, pp. 115–132.

Halliday, M.A.K. (1978) *Language as Social Semiotics: The Social Interpretation of Language and Meaning,* London, Edward Arnold.

Halliday, M.A.K., Hasan, R. (1985) *Language, Context and Text. Aspects of Language in a Social-Semiotic Perspective,* Oxford, Oxford UP.

Harrison, C. (2020) 'The truth is we're watching each other': Voiceover Narration as 'Split Self' Presentation in *The Handmaid's Tale* TV Series, *Language and Literature,* 29:1, pp. 22–38.

Hutcheon, L. with O'Flynn, S. (2013) *A Theory of Adaptation,* 2nd ed., London/New York, Routledge.

Ingham, M. (2017) Popular Song and Adaptation, in T. Leitch (ed.) *The Oxford Handbook of Adaptation Studies,* Oxford, Oxford U.P., 325–339.

Inglis, I. (2012) Music into Movies: The Film of the Song, in D. Cartmell (ed.) *A Companion to Literature, Film, and Adaptation,* Oxford, Blackwell, pp. 312–329.

Kalinak, K. (2010) *Film Music: A Very Short Introduction,* Oxford, Oxford UP.

Kozloff, S. (1988) *Invisible Storytellers: Voice-Over Narration in American Fiction Film,* Berkeley, University of California Press.

Kozloff, S. (2000) *Overhearing Film Dialogue,* Berkeley, University of California Press.

Kress, G., van Leeuwen, T. (2001) *Multimodal Discourse: The Modes and Media of Contemporary Communication,* London, Arnold.

Kress, G., van Leeuwen, T. (2006) *Reading Images: The Grammar of Visual Design,* 2nd ed., London/New York, Routledge.

McIntyre, D. (2008) Integrating Multimodal Analysis and the Stylistics of Drama: A Multimodal Perspective on Ian McKellen's *Richard III*, *Language and Literature*, 17:4, pp. 309–334.

Nørgaard, N. (2014) Multimodality and Stylistics, in M. Burke (ed.) *The Routledge Handbook to Stylistics*, op. cit., pp. 471–484.

Pillière, L. (2014) Crossing New Frontiers? Investigating Style from a Multimodal Perspective, *Études de stylistique anglaise*, 7, pp. 99–120.

Robinson, G. (2012) "Writing for the Silent Screen", D. Cartmell (ed.) *A Companion to Literature, Film, and Adaptation*, op. cit., pp. 33–51.

Toolan, M. (2014) Stylistics and Film, in M. Burke (ed.) *The Routledge Handbook to Stylistics*, London/New York, Routledge, pp. 455–470.

van Leeuwen, T. (1999) *Speech, Music, Sound*, London, Macmillan.

van Leeuwen, T. (2011) *The Language of Colour*, London/New York, Routledge.

3   Short Canadian Films

Boys and Girls

Released in 1983, the short film *Boys and Girls* was produced by the small company Atlantis Films Limited in Association with the Canadian Broadcasting Corporation. It received an Academy Award for the best story-live-action film and signalled the beginning of director Don McBrearty's television career (Thacker 2011, p. 407). With a screenplay by Joe Wiesenfeld and music by Louis Natale, the film adaptation has been made freely available online. The short story of the same title first appeared on December 12, 1964, in the pages of the *Montrealer*, a monthly magazine addressing the English-speaking Montreal community, which published five stories by Munro from 1961 to 1965 (Ue 2014, p. 178). It was then anthologised in the first collection by the Canadian writer, *Dance of the Happy Shades* (1968) and, subsequently, included in collections of selected stories from her various volumes.

Told by an unnamed, first-person narrator, the adapted text revolves around the everyday life of a family, living in a farmhouse in a small-town community in Southwestern Ontario, raising horses and foxes. As the story focaliser, the daughter perceives gender-based inequalities in her parents' approach and relationships to their son and daughter. The eleven-year-old protagonist helps her father bring water to the foxes and rake the just-cut grass into piles, activities she finds rewarding. However, the family expects her to attend to "more female" duties within the kitchen walls, like peeling peaches or chopping onions. The short story, in Ventura's words (1992, p. 80), "bring[s] into focus gender role stereotyping and the limitations enforced on the girl as she grows into adolescence". The climax of the story is when the protagonist does not close the farmhouse gate and lets the old horse Flora escape, thus obliging her father to chase the animal across the surrounding countryside.

DOI: 10.4324/9781003183846-4

The protagonist of the twenty-five-minute adaptation is thirteen-year-old Margaret, played by Megan Follows: she is, thus, two years older than Munro's protagonist and has a name. Other actors include Clare Coulter as Margaret's mother, David Fox as her father, Ian Heath as her brother Laird, and Winnie Farrell as her grandmother. Living in a farmhouse in a small-town Ontario community, the girl longs for the freedom of the outside world but is instead forced to help her mother in the oppressive kitchen. By letting Flora escape before she could be killed by her farmer father, the girl "resist[s] both obedience to her father and the gender role imposed upon her as a girl" (Ue 2014, p. 178).

Margaret is a recurring character across the scenes, especially when these are set in her bedroom and in the barn. She is primarily depicted alone. When portrayed with other characters, she appears generally with her younger brother Laird, in the barn, in the barnyard, and in their bedroom. Their co-presence corroborates what is mentioned in the title: a relation between boys and girls (Ventura 1992, p. 84). Sometimes Margaret is with the mother and the grandmother in the kitchen.

In order to represent Margaret, McBrearty predominantly adopts the close-up as a size-of-frame technique, thus shaping an intimate social distance between the protagonist and the audience. Consistently, an eye angle is primarily used to frame perspective, to position interactive participants on the same level in terms of power dynamics. Overall, the film relies on perspective and size of frame to reveal interiority, to establish intimacy, and to enact focalisation.

The introspective dimension of the film narrative is also evoked through the trope of the mirror, a pervasive feature in several film adaptations of Munro's stories. A central scene of *Boys and Girls* (13:12–13:58) captures Margaret in her poorly illuminated bedroom, looking at her refracted image on the bureau mirror. She is sitting down, her posture static, her gaze profound. Laird is also in the room, off-screen, partially reflected by the mirror. Self-mirroring does not look like a perceptive process, but a cognitive one: Margaret is not controlling her appearance, but scrutinising her identity. As heterotopic space (Foucault 1966), the mirror does not reduplicate the self but reveals tensions and contradictions; it allows the text to negotiate intimacy, agency, and diegetic patterns. Less a mere domestic piece of furniture than a narrative trigger, it ultimately engenders Margaret's reaction to paternal law when she lets Flora escape.

As mentioned above, the film foregrounds Margaret's personal growth, from self-legitimation to challenging the paternal mindset.

It opens and closes with a two-individual shot featuring Margaret and her brother Laird. In the opening scene, the two are watching their father and the hired man who kill Mack, an old horse, whose meat will be used to feed the silver foxes. Firmly holding Laird's arms and looking into his eyes, Margaret uses a patronising tone to tell him: "Laird, it's something they have to do. Better to see and to know" (01:20–01:46). The film ends with Margaret and Laird outside in the yard: she in sitting in the father's truck, while he is outside the truck, in a lower position. They are discussing the fact that Margaret has opened the farmhouse gate and let the old horse Flora escape. A reverse shot shows Margaret telling her brother, in a challenging tone: "But, you know, Laird? They are never gonna catch me!" Through the interplay of voice-in, position, and posture, the film expresses Margaret's challenge to the patriarchal system. In the circular compositional scheme of the film, the two-individual shot is presented by McBrearty through patterns of repetition with variation, which foregrounds and celebrates Margaret's growth.

In order to show the development of awareness in Margaret, the director manipulates the process of adaptation using anticipation and addition in the opening and closing of two-individual shots, respectively. As a matter of fact, the location of the film's opening scene does not reflect that of the corresponding scene in the short story, which occurs later in the narrative. This dislocation foregrounds Margaret's change across time: she initially legitimises and later rejects the social system. The concluding segment, instead, has been added to the storyline, as Ue notices (2014, p. 182). This addition suggests that Margaret does challenge the social system represented by her father, while her relationship with her brother seems to show reconciliation. If the short story leaves the additive conjunction "and" of the title fraught with unresolved conflict, the film seems to restore the literal meaning promised by grammar books. Overall, as Ue argues (2014, p. 182), the film appears more optimistic than the short story in its tempered conclusion, which is another frequent trait of screen adaptations of Munro's stories.

Gender andlas Space Representation

Throughout the film, Margaret is forced to help her mother inside the oppressive kitchen, while longing for the freedom of the outside world. In order to explore gender roles and constraints, the director relies on a systemically polarised representation of space. Tom Ue notices (2014, p. 175) a series of semiotic contrasts between the inside and outside, between lit and dark areas, between cold and warm colours and light. These denounce "the narrator's incarceration" (Ue 2014, p. 175) and raise issues of gender and identity. Ventura (1992) identifies the same logical mechanism in the short story and argues that the locations are profoundly gendered: female and male spaces are defined by rigid boundaries and categories. This dichotomous system has the women being constrained within the domestic walls, whereas the men live in the outside space. Gender conflict, through the opposition between domesticity and the outside world, is expressed in the film both within and across shots.

The audio-visual artefact relies on the *mise en scène* to suggest values of oppression and freedom within the shot. Kitchen scenes are generally taken from an oblique angle using medium size. Different layers of depth, as well as vectors projected by gaze or action, reveal mutual relationships between the human participants, primarily women. In the domestic space, light is never diffuse: there is a contrast between lit and dark areas. To the opposite, in the yard, long shots encode ample space and diffuse natural light engenders a sense of freedom. Ue argues (2014, p. 180) that McBrearty shoots exterior scenes in an expansive and liberating way, providing the setting for Margaret and Laird to run and play games. The director relies on size of frame to physically "expand" the natural environment and uses the characters' movements to express the fruition of that exterior space. Even working in such a space seems to Margaret pleasant and rewarding, however hard and tiring it may be.

The oppositional stance is not neat, as in-between spaces are also depicted on screen. Bedroom scenes are poorly lit, in order to express introspection and speculation. In contrast, effect lighting is used in the barn, to project a symbolic relation between Margaret and the old horse Flora. Similarly, space representation is not only concerned with symbolic discourse upon gender. In his accurate depiction of the society of the time, the director seems to show a documentary aim. Scenes in the kitchen, in the foxes' pen, in the shed show all objects, utensils, appliances in detail and in a foregrounded position: attention is given to hard work being a crucial part of rural life (Ue 2014, p. 181). If accuracy in the *mise en scène* is undeniable, it is not the ultimate aim of the film's meaning-making system.

All these intra and inter-shot strategies serve to depict space as deriving from subjective perception. Such a view reflects Munro's own approach, where physical position in the short story is

Table 3.1 Indoor and outdoor-based scenes

Scene	Setting	Action
1	Barn	Margaret and Laird see a horse being shot in the barnyard
2	Kitchen	Margaret and her mother are doing housework while the mother tells stories
3	The foxes' pen	Margaret and Laird are feeding the silver foxes
4	Shed	Margaret and father have a chat while grinding the meat for the silver foxes
5	The foxes' pen	Margaret wants to help the father brush the foxes' fur
6	Barn	While pitching hay, Margaret is called by her mother
7	Kitchen	While checking the laundry, Margaret's mother talks about lace
8	Barnyard	While Margaret is collecting water, the men leave with a tractor
9	Kitchen	Women talk in the kitchen
10	Yard	Margaret and Laird have fun together
11	Kitchen	Women discuss gender roles and duties
12	Yard	Margaret and Laird discuss gender differences
13	Barn	The profound connection between Flora and Margaret
14	Bedroom	Margaret in front of a mirror talks to Laird off-space
15	Kitchen	Margaret and her parents talk about the horses
16	Barn	The profound connection between Margaret and Flora
17	Yard	Flora escapes with Margaret's help
18	Kitchen	Margaret with her mother
19	Bedroom	Margaret alone
20	Yard	Margaret, Laird, and the men
21	Bedroom	Margaret alone
22	Yard	Men are satisfied with themselves after reaching Flora
23	Kitchen	The family is having dinner
24	Yard	Dialogue between Margaret and Laird in a truck

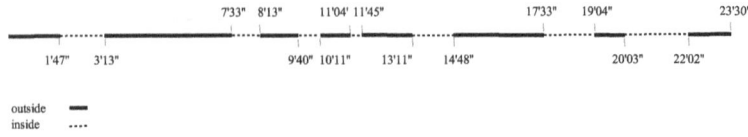

Figure 3.1 Indoor and outdoor-based scenes.

multisensorially defined, as the filter for the perception and representation of reality: "I walked on stubble in the earlier evening, aware of the reddening skies, the entering silences, of fall" (Munro 1997, p. 118). In a passage that evokes filmic discourse, the moving character captures the fluidity of the surrounding environment, motion being both in the subject and in the object of perception. Awareness entwines both the multisensorial stimulus and the cognitive elaboration. Moreover, the surrounding space always projects personal emotions, feelings, moods, as we can read elsewhere: "I hated the hot dark kitchen in summer, the green blinds and the flypapers, the same old oilcloth table and wavy mirror and bumpy linoleum" (Munro 1997, p. 119). In the short story, space representation encodes physical perspective, multisensorial perception, as well as emotional and affective concerns. All these aspects are convincingly rendered in the film.

Besides being intersemiotically realised within the *mise en scène*, tension, confinement, incarceration are also projected in terms of sequential composition at the level of editing, through the alternation of indoor and outdoor-based scenes, as Table. 3.1 and Figure 3.1 show.

As the Table and Image demonstrate, the film relies on composition to stress the distinction and suggest the tension between the two domains. It alternates between exterior and interior scenes along the sequential film axis with the connotation that they are, respectively, male and female spaces. Besides performing this semiotic function, this type of organisation adds rhythm to the film narrative and challenges the compact structure of the short story, anchored around the protagonist. Notably, in this early adaptation, the director tries to deconstruct Munro's highly cohesive text, whereas later films move in the opposite direction, making loose stories more compact.

Overall, this short film maintains a strict connection to the adapted text and shows profound continuity of plot, setting, and themes. Primarily concerned with the psychological dimension and with gender-related enquiries, McBrearty's film proves that the semiotic system of film can express and negotiate interiority, contradicting widespread clichés. Interestingly, interiority and gender are here symbolically explored through patterns of space representation, both through the *mise en scène* and editing. It seems that the film seeks to express the main concerns of the literary work, relying on the affordances of the audio-visual system.

Thanks for the Ride

Produced by the National Film Board of Canada, *Thanks for the Ride* (1983) was written and directed by John Kent Harrison. The adapted story of the same title was first published in the *Tamarack Review* in the winter of 1957 and then included in Munro's first collection *Dance of the Happy Shades* (1968). Set in Ontario, it is about two cousins from the city, Dick and George and, unusually for Munro, the narrator is one of these men, Dick, "just out of high-school" (Munro 1997, p. 46). The cousins go out with two young women, Adelaide and Lois, whom they met in Mission Creek, a little town on the shores of Lake Huron. Given their differences in terms of social class and education, the young men and women experience profound isolation during the evening they spend together. The short story ends with Lois's cry: "Thanks for the Ride!", according to Bigot and Lanone (2014, p. 127) "a way of regaining partial control over the scene as the men leave, of having the last laugh, the last word".

The twenty-eight-minute adaptation features Lesley Donaldson as Vicky, Melissa Bell as LoreAnn, Peter Kranz as George, and Carl Maroote as David and relies on an expensive car to signal the higher social status of the protagonist, renamed David in the film. The opening scene shows David in a garage, asking his father if he can drive his car. Father and son are staying in a luxury villa overlooking Lake Huron, celebrated through a couple of suggestive long shots. The young man then exits the garage, crosses the yard, and reaches the living room, where he takes his jacket and heads out in the car. He first stops to pick up his cousin George, his mate in this adventure. Together, they drive towards Mission Creek, whose name is shown by an old street sign gone awry that the camera lingers on. The use of such visual inserts in the adaptation is reminiscent of the use of signs in Munrovian texts. Events narrated in this long opening unit (00:00–03:32) are not present in the adapted story, as if the director wanted to provide background information on the characters and the setting, as well as to offer a clear and recognisable beginning for the adventure. The ouverture offers the audience an interpretative lens for the whole narrative, that of social class privilege.

The next cinematographic sequence, corresponding to the actual beginning of the short story, is set at the Live bar in Mission Creek. Here the two boys meet LoreAnn, a beautiful young woman ("pale, almost ugly, [with] an inexplicable aura of sexuality" (Munro 1997, p. 48)), whom George courts and invites out for a ride. They leave the bar and George asks if LoreAnn has a friend. On their way, they unexpectedly see Vicky, the friend they were looking for. The young woman reluctantly accepts the invitation to join the group, but asks to go home beforehand, in order to change her clothes. While driving, David sometimes checks the rear window of his car in order to look at Vicky and LoreAnn sitting in the back seat. Not only a strategy for projecting the young man's focalisation, this symbolic gesture also reveals David's privileged perspective in terms of gender and social class, as epitomised by his car. Meanwhile, the rear window expresses George's vain attempts to understand the young woman, to fit in. In the end, he is also the victim of social and gender imbalance.

The two couples stop near a barn where Vicky and David have an animated discussion about summer relationships between richer boys coming from the city and poorer local girls. Animation mutates into sexual intercourse inside the barn, the boy's sexual initiation. The camera indulges on their bodies, accompanied by instrumental music, whereas the short story leaves a blank space after mentioning the place of their intimate encounter (Munro's readers are informed later that Lois, generally cold, detached and scornful was a "mystic of love"; Munro 1997, p. 58). Then they go back home, leave the girls and Vicky yells: "Thanks for the ride!" Whereas the short story ends with Lois's cry, the film ends with the boys driving back home. The car lights are glaring brightly in the darkness of the night.

David operates as both the protagonist and the focaliser in this short film. The character's relevance is not only due to his pervasive and strategic presence (across the whole film, including front and end positions) but also through foregrounding techniques of representation like the close-up. His socially privileged family background is symbolised by his father's expensive car. The vehicle is on screen as the setting for four long sequences: the opening ride to the Live bar (01:37–03:32); the ride to Vicky's house (06:37–09:21); the ride to the isolated barn in the field, where David and Vicky have sex (12:46–15:02); the final ride back home (24:04–27:11). Several shots represent the car itself as the main represented participant, like the opening shot itself in the garage, and numerous long shots showing the car crossing the bush. The powerful visual metaphor is then used as a framing device to open and close the film narrative. David's relationship with the car seems to shape and crystallise his personality more than his interaction with several characters throughout the film narrative, like his father, Vicky, Vicky's mother and George.

After leaving the Live bar, as already mentioned, David and George meet LoreAnn's friend Vicky at 07:27. She is walking home but they invite her to join them. Before accepting, she asks to go home and change her dress. They stop at Vicky's house and, while Vicky gets ready in her bedroom, David meets her mother, a talk-ative and intrusive woman who is very interested in David's family and who tells stories about her own family. The stop highlights the different social background between Vicky and David's families and the young woman operates as his female and poorer correlate. A range of multimodal strategies depict Vicky's family, house, clothes, and invite the spectator's emphatic gaze. Spectators can en-gage with this elusive and detached character, frequently captured through intense close-ups. They can also enter her bedroom, while she is getting ready for the ride (David's house was only shown through the public spaces of the garage, garden, and living room). The gradual foregrounding of Vicky's character culminates in her challenging cry towards the end of the film. David and Vicky then leave the house, join the other couple and continue the ride.

Like the short story, the film operates a shift in focalisation and reverses the relation spectators entertain with the male and film characters. The initial protagonist and focaliser, David plays a role prescribed by his gender and social class and expresses his identity via his father's car. Vicky, to the opposite, resorts to her challenging cry as a subversive act, to reject the position assigned to girls with the "rituals of the sex date" (Bigot and Lanone 2014, p. 38). The shift in focalisation is suggested by the use of the mirror trope, fea-turing repetition and variation. Two scenes centred on David first and on Vicky later (dis)connect the two characters. Positioned at the beginning of the film (01:13–01:37), the first segment is set in the living room: David quickly controls his image in the mirror before going out to pick up George. He approves his refracted image with a self-satisfied smile. Later in the film, with two embedded units showing David and Vicky's mother, the camera captures Vicky in her bedroom (10:34–10:50; 11:23–11:34). Sitting in front of her mirror, she is putting on some make-up. In the introspective scene, Vicky is indulging in her intimate thoughts and feelings. The units are also different in duration and rhythm, David's mirror scene being shorter and quicker (also because the embedded units in Vicky's scene produce a slowing-down effect). The two scenes signal and mark David and Vicky's profound differences in terms of personality and social status and contribute to the previously discussed reversal of their interpersonal relationship. The film, thus, convincingly, represents and negotiates intimacy and distance to underscore the intersectional discussion about gender and social class.

Film Music Framing Theme, Time, and Tone

From the multimodal perspective, attention should be drawn to the film's soundscape, as the film music is extremely relevant within the film's meaning-making system. The introduction and second sequence end with a piece of music in the figure position: *Hello, Young Lovers* by Frank Sinatra (this was actually a show tune, originally composed for the 1951 Rodgers and Hammerstein musical *The King and I*. End titles credit MCA Records). The lyrics frame the romantic motif of the film narrative:

> Hello young lovers whoever you are
> I hope your troubles are few
> All my good wishes go with you tonight
> I've been in love like you
> Be brave young lovers and follow your star
> Be brave and faithful and true
> Cling very close to each other tonight
> I've been in love like you

The song's message expresses the perspective of a mature person, who has lived and who has loved. By adopting a second-person plural pronoun, the adult man in the film's song offers his best wishes to the young boys in the film narrative, identifying with them ("I've been in love like you") and recommending they be brave ("Be brave young lovers and follow your star"). In the *mise en scène*, the film's music is superimposed upon the film's images and seems to offer a recommendation to the characters and a line of interpretation to the audience. The facts that the song is not a score but has been "recycled" and that the singer is a celebrity further reinforce the idea that the song holds a prominent position in the signifying system and that it enacts a sort of control over the narrative. The singing voice may be read as that of an experienced heterodiegetic narrator who casts a nostalgic and paternalistic gaze upon events. The narrative stance is, in part, reminiscent of many Munrovian narrators, who engage with the characters from a later position in time, characterised by maturity and awareness. Most narrators in Munro are, however, homodiegetic. When adapted for the screen, these stances are elsewhere represented through the voice-over technique (e.g., in *Connection* and *Lives of Girls and Women*).

This soundtrack is present in two of the film's sequences: first, with David and George in the car on the ride towards Mission Creek (02:29–03:16), second and later, when Vicky and David are sitting in the car alone (14:12–14:42). In the first case, only the first two stanzas of Sinatra's song are sung, in the second case only the first one. This strategy invites spectators to pay attention to the foregrounded lyrics and to consider them part of the film's semiosis. In the first unit, David is driving the car, while George is standing, since the roof is open, the wind in his hair, his arms raised to sign victory. The piece of music follows George's suggestion "Let's get some ladies!", thus inscribing a phallogocentric discourse within the motif of the story. In the second unit, David switches the radio off but Vicky says she likes it. The song is stopped when the voice sings the words "be brave", maybe signalling David's uneasiness with the role of the "brave young lover". Then, David asks Vicky if she prefers the music on, but she replies: "It doesn't matter". When the soundtrack is heard for second time, it is fraught with tension, as the atmosphere between David and Vicky is already tense. Hence, the use of the soundtrack shows patterns of repetition with variation: it is first associated with euphoria and then with disillusion.

Overall, *Hello, young lovers* is present in the first part of the film, while the second part is accompanied by slow, melancholic, and discontinuous instrumental music (10:35–end), so that the two music systems are not neatly separated but overlap in the central part. The meaning potential of the song can mostly be ascribed to its words, whereas the instrumental music mainly relies on melody to contribute to the film's meaning potential. In other terms, the soundtrack mainly operates at the ideational level, as it conveys a message, whereas the instrumental music mainly works interpersonally, as mood creator. It engenders a melancholic atmosphere, reinforcing the sense of isolation pervading the narrative. In spite of these predominant functions, the two sound elements operate in a complementary way within the unfolding narrative: Sinatra's song signals the narrative's opening in terms of wishes, expectations, potential, energy, whereas the sad background music marks the release of energy, the awareness of limits, tensions, reality. Moreover, the musical elements also play a cohesive function, as they hold the narrative together.

Overall, *Thanks for the Ride* seems to adopt a line of continuity while, at the same time, allowing for a screen transformation of Munro's short story. The film is effective in capturing the character's introspective depth and the interpersonal tension between David and Vicky, as well as in shifting focalisation. Multimodal resources are effectively combined to render the psychological atmosphere, the pervasive sense of isolation, and entrapment of the narrative palpable. However, the film adopts several strategies in order to make the narrative more explicit and more cohesive:

- The film's song foregrounds the theme of adolescent love pervading the story and shapes an external narratorial stance that allows for control of the narrative, also adding a nostalgic tone.
- The addition of the opening sequence clarifies the socio-cultural context in which events take place, and the visual metaphor of the car reinforces the notion of privileged socio-economic status, which provides the lens for the romantic adventure.
- Evoking *Boys and Girls* the connected opening and closing scenes add a circular frame to the film narrative, with the visual metaphor of the car in the opening- and end-position and the film's music operating as cohesive devices.
- While the short story shows an elliptical blank space, the camera indulges in David and Vicky's bodies having sex in the barn.

Unlike Munro's reader, the viewer is accompanied throughout the narrative and is given all the elements s/he needs to follow and understand the plot and the narrative.

All about *Connection*

Set in an elegant Vancouver district, the film *Connection* (1986) narrates the tensions between Maureen and her husband Richard, a successful and arrogant lawyer. When the couple receives a phone call from Iris, an exuberant relative Maureen has not seen for years, Maureen invites her for dinner. The phone call, the arrival of this woman, and the sharing of some memories from the past allow a second parallel story, as well as a second temporal dimension, to unfold. The latter revolves around a summer visit that four unmarried cousins, including Iris, had paid to Maureen's family in Dalgleish, their small hometown in rural Ontario: a joyful time, full of stories, songs, laughs, and even a concert. Quite differently, the Vancouver dinner is consumed in an unpleasant atmosphere, as Iris' vibrant stories clash with the married couple's tension. After Richard's harsh comments upon Iris's departure, Maureen throws a plate with a piece of lemon meringue pie at him.

Produced by Atlantis Films and the National Film Board of Canada, *Connection* is freely available on the YouTube platform. Written by Kelly Rebar, directed by Wolf König, with music composed by Harry Freedman, the twenty-four-minute adaptation features Kate Trotter (Maureen), Patricia Hamilton (Iris), and Tom Butler (Richard). It brings Munro's "Connection" to the screen as part of a double short story devoted to her family history, entitled "Chaddeleys & Flemings", collected in *The Moons of Jupiter* (1982). In the first part, "Connection", the unnamed female protagonist retraces the maternal side, populated by a long list of sociable and noisy open cousins—including Iris; the second part, "The Stone in the Field", centres on the paternal side, composed of reserved and old-fashioned aunts. Not only does the film significantly omit the paternal side of the family as it centres on the first of the twin stories, it also limits a long story about the British side of the maternal family, which is prominent in the short story and fascinates the cousins.

Set in the small town of Dalgleish, in rural Western Ontario, the first part of Munro's literary text is followed by a second part, set in Capilano Heights, Vancouver. The unnamed protagonist in the first part becomes an adult married woman, mother of two daughters, in the second part. Both sections develop around a visit by family members: the first revolves around four cousins visiting the family, and the second narrates of Iris's visit to the protagonist and her "critical and repressive" husband (Hooper 2008, p. 66). The story culminates when the protagonist throws a plate with a piece of lemon meringue pie at her husband, after Richard hostile behaviour towards the cousin. This "both humorous and sad scene" (Thacker 2011, p. 233) symbolically signals the end of their marriage. As the narrator sustains, the problem is that of a connection to one's personal past, to one's family history: "[Richard] wanted me amputated from that past which seemed to him such shabby

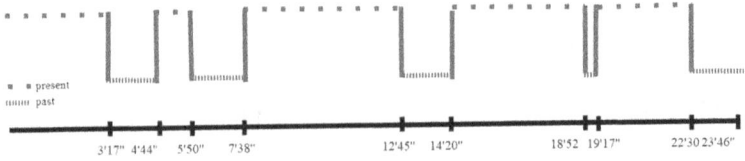

Figure 3.2 Flashback units in connection.

baggage" (Munro 1995, p. 13). Hence, it is with the resurfacing of the non-amputated past that the story ends, with a flashback unit about the four cousins' visit as a form of resistance to the amputation (Rasporich 1990, p. 149).

The literary and filmic texts are formally and semiotically concerned with compositional strategies used to connect present and past. It is indeed in relation to present and past scenes and sequences that the film adaptation performs the most significant intersemiotic processes of manipulation. In the literary text, past and present are sequentially organised (past, present, past), while in the film, they are simultaneous and layered, with flashbacks embedded within the present diegesis. The past about the summer visit in Dalgleish is narrated through five distinct flashbacks integrated into the present narrative strand about the dinner in Vancouver. Analeptic sections account for a total of 4:56 out of 23:46 minutes (03:17–4:44; 05:50–7:32; 12:45–14:20; 18:52–19:17; 22:30–23:46). Figure 3.2 illustrates their distribution in the film narrative.

In the film, the story is told by a homodiegetic narrator, through a pervasive voice-over. Belonging to Maureen, the female voice speaks from a later temporal position, many years after the Vancouver dinner, and at a time when the woman has achieved detachment, maturity, and awareness. Hence, the device enables the director to negotiate the relationship between the narrated and narrating self, the past of the story, and the present of storytelling. Overall, there are eight voice-over units, all located in the first part of the cinematographic narrative. The first one opens the film itself and anticipates the conclusion of the story, namely the end of the marriage: "I had wondered if there would be a moment when I would know my marriage to Richard was over. Do these moments come to you or do you come to them? It turned out it was both" (00:00–00:52). The multiple tenses create layered temporal lines: the narrator can travel back and forth in time and can meditate upon events from her present vantage point.

After only mentioning him in the first voice-over unit, the second chunk describes Richard in terms of social position, education, and attitude: "Good old Richard: he never did let you forget his pedigree: Upper Canada College all's good Hall Harvard Law School, old Ontario money" (01:37–01:51). The sarcastic tone embeds evaluation components within the descriptive text (e.g., "good old Richard", "all's good", "old Ontario money"). The wealthy man is mocked for building his identity on his financial and social privilege. Moreover, he overtly displays his snobbish attitude towards the wife's background:

> As for me, if I ever mentioned my family or Dalgleish, Ontario, where I grew up, Richard would almost wince as though I'd said something slightly obscene. He found it hard to live with the fact that my people were just farmers, poor farmers.
>
> (01:56–02:32)

This third voice-over unit ends proleptically: "The end of my marriage came unexpectedly as so many of these things do, with a phone call from someone I hadn't seen in years". In its last part, this third unit announces and triggers the phone call itself. The string "unexpectedly as so many of these things do" signals a generalisation, allowed by the temporal distance and mediation upon the event. On the phone, Maureen and her cousin start talking about the past.

The first temporal shift occurs during the phone call itself, when Maureen tries to remember how many years have passed since her last meeting with her relative: "It must be at least 18 years, Iris, because I was still in high school when you all came to visit". The sentence activates the flashback about the visit itself. The first analepsis (03:44–05:11) features three voice-over units and centres on the "maiden ladies". In a fractured style, Maureen lists the women, their jobs and places of residence: "Cousin Iris was a nurse, a head nurse. Cousin Flora was a teacher. She was from Winnipeg. Cousin Winifred was a lady accountant. She was from Edmonton" (03:34–03:50). Soon after, she clarifies the group name used to refer to the women: "Maiden ladies, they were called. 'Old maids' was too thin a term, it wouldn't cover them" (04:05–04:15). She then presents the event: the visit paid by the maiden ladies to their cousin and her family:

> They all came to stay with us one summer. They came to our house because my mother was the only married one, with a

house big enough to accommodate everyone and because she couldn't afford to go to see them.

(04:20–04:35)

After this, the narrative goes back to the main diegetic level, with Maureen preparing the dinner and checking the table. In a new introspective voice-over unit (06:02–06:30), the narrator's thoughts focus on the key term: "connection":

> Connection, that's what it was all about. Mother's cousins provided us all with the connection to the real and prodigal and dangerous world they knew how to get on in it. They had made it take notice. They knew how to deal with taxi drivers and train conductors.

Again, the voice-over enables the narrator to cast a synthetic gaze ("that's what it was all about") over the situation, to state an argument (the cousins offer social connections), and to provide evidence to support it (the cousins' expertise with the real and dangerous world's dynamics and mechanisms).

The voice-over is thus used pervasively and multifunctionally across the whole narrative. The technique has a primary ideational metafunction, as it gives information about people and facts. Interestingly, information progressively becomes more intimate across the film narrative, as there is a movement from exteriority to interiority. For instance, the last voice-over section confesses Maureen's intimate expectations about the dinner. She wanted Iris to be acceptable and accepted but she also wanted to impress her guest and display her acquired social status and lifestyle:

> I wanted this visit to go well. I wanted cousin Iris to be a relative nobody needed to be ashamed of. And I'm afraid I also wanted Richard and his money and our house to impress Iris and forever lift me out of the category of poor relation.

(07:50–08:10)

In the thematised position, the cluster "And I'm afraid" inscribes the contradictions in her expectations, hiding her insecurities at the time of the dinner and revealing her achieved awareness and sense of guilt at the time of narrating.

The voice-over, also, operates interpersonally, as it establishes and negotiates conflict between represented participants: it "disconnects" Maureen and Richard. Most interestingly, in operates intrapersonally, as it "disconnects" the narrated self in the past from the narrating self in the present. Meanwhile, it acts as a significant compositional strategy, as it "connects" the present and past sections and it weaves the first part of the cinematographic narrative together, making the story fruition smooth. From the viewpoint of adaptation, numerous voice-over units tend to reproduce the adapted text verbatim, thus to signal and mark a fil rouge between adapted text and adaptation. The voice-over may be heard as echoing Munro's voice within the film's multimodal narrative.

Overall, this film profoundly relies on verbal language in all its forms. If the voice-over negotiates the tension between narrated and narrating self, the voice-in is used to cross present and past temporal plans. In fact, transitions from the present to the past are clearly triggered by verbal cues. After the visit instance mentioned above, the second trigger is the family name "Chaddeley", uttered by Richard with condescension when he hands the phone to Maureen: "she [Iris] sounds like a Chaddeley to me". The verbal cue prompts the retrospective scene with the cousins interpreting baby Maureen's facial traits: "What do you think Winifred: is she a Chaddeley or a Fleming?" The transition operates through noun repetition and connotation reversal: unlike Richard's negative connotation, the cousins assign positive meanings to the family name. The flashback ends when Grace, the mother, asks Maureen: "Maureen get me that jug of lemonade, would you?" A close-up on an elegant crystal glass brings the narrative back to the present and to Maureen's nostalgia. The jug-glass interplay enacts a verbal-visual connection based on difference in terms of atmosphere: past joy and present tension.

Further temporal leaps are prompted by Iris' stories during the dinner in the present that evoke Iris' own stories during the summer visit of the past. From a logico-semantic perspective, the last shift mirrors the first one: Maureen asks Iris if she remembers the concert, she organised during that summer in Dalgleish, with distinct roles assigned to every participant. The flashback shows the merry concert itself, with Grace standing on her head, upside-down, in her husband's trousers. Enacted at the level of dialogue, though lexical items ("Chaddeley", "jug of lemonade", "concert"), all flashbacks in the film are also clearly anticipated by slow motion and signalled through the adoption of archaic recording devices, which project blurred and opaque images.

If voice-over and voice-in cross temporal plans, the soundtrack only inhabits the flashback scenes. The third (12:45–14:20) and the fifth (22:30–23:46) analeptic units feature a popular song present in the adapted text:

> Row, row, row your boat
> Gently down the stream
> Merrily, merrily, merrily, merrily
> Life is but a dream.

The American nursery rhyme is initiated by Iris, and then the other women around her join in. The first scene is very short (14:12–14:18), but the song continues later, in the closing section of the film. If in its first part it shapes the "merry" atmosphere surrounding the women's gathering in Dalgleish, in the second part and end position, it achieves an ironic effect, as it creates tension between the "sweet childhood memory" scenes and the "sour adult present" ones (Thacker 2011, p. 372). In this vein, the "dream" of the song may be read ironically, as Maureen apparently lives a dream life in Vancouver, but is actually unhappy. Unlike the song in *Thanks for the Ride* that frames the narrator's stance, time and tone, this song provides the audience with a hermeneutical cue.

The conclusion of the short story draws us back to the song and to the progressive silencing of the female voices: "the song is thinning out, you can hear the two voices striving [...] Then the one voice alone, one of them singing on, gamely, to the finish" (Munro 1995, p. 18). As Redekop observes (1992, p. 163), "Munro uses print to act like a slow motion". This solution already invites the cinematographic adaptation and provides a tip for the key technique to be adopted. However, if the rhythm of narrative slows down, full stops fracture and fragment items: "One voice in which there is an unexpected note of entreaty, of warning, as it hangs the five separate words on the air. *Life is*. Wait. *But a*. Now, wait. *Dream*" (Munro 1995, p. 18). Thacker (2011, p. 372) foregrounds the use of the term "warning" in this passage and claims that the lyrics operate as a "warning" within the whole narrative. The yearning for connections can only be, in Munro, a disconnected and disconnecting one.

As the title suggests, this film is about connections, expressed both thematically and formally. From a thematic perspective, connections are first made to the real, outside urban, mobile world symbolised by the cousins during their summer visit. "Connection" is also to be intended to portray a broader and intricate web of family relations. They are, then, connections with the past, when the narrator was in high school and lived in a poor rural milieu.

Enacted by Iris's stories, the connection with the past implies a disconnection from the alienating present. Connections are also to the self, to a profound, contradictory, complex self, not to the one developed and honed to please the husband. From a formal viewpoint, connections are made by the temporal diegetic lines the short story deploys and the use of flashbacks to break the unfolding narrative. They are thus related to the narrative sequences, namely the story fragments the film is divided into. They also impact the audio and visual semiotic systems, co-occurring and integrating across the scenes through a range of strategies like the slow motion and cross-fade, the voice-over and soundtrack. In short, the film may be read as a longing for connections, and this motif is developed consistently at all narrative levels and systemically through several narrative strategies.

Overall, the adaptation process implies a structural re-organisation of the narrative, with the parallel unfolding of the present and past temporal levels. The centrality given to the dinner, with embedded scenes from the past, implies the compression of the family tree discourse. In this way, the film architecture turns out to be more compact than the literary one. The cohesive effect is corroborated by the voice-over strategy, which leads, holds, and controls the narrative, also stressing the theme of the story. In the second part of the film, cohesion is achieved with an audio strategy, the women's song, which compliments and balances the voice-over as a structuring device. Alongside the voice-over and lyrics, verbal language operates as memory-trigger, when verbal cues are adopted to prompt retrospection scenes. The film adaptation, overall, systemically relies on the verbal mode in its meaning-making system (voice-over, voice-in, lyrics) and thus reinforces its connection to the adapted text.

To sum up, the three early and short adaptations addressed in this chapter, *Boys and Girls*, *Thanks for the Ride*, and *Connection* raise and develop some thematic issues that will appear in film adaptations across the following decades: intrapersonal and interpersonal conflict, as well as socio-cultural inequalities and their impact on everyday life. The films also deploy some significant formal and semiotic solutions that allow for screen adaptations of Munro's stories, including the voice-over, songs, and editing techniques. These demonstrate different ways to engage with primary concerns posed by the adaptation challenge, including the narrator's stance, temporal horizons, and narrative composition.

References

Bigot, C., Lanone, C. (2014) *Sunlight and Shadows, Past and Present. Alice Munro's Dance of the Happy Shades*, Paris, PUF.

Foucault, M. (1966) *Les mots et les choses*, Paris, Gallimard.

Hooper, B. (2008) *The Fiction of Alice Munro. An Appreciation*, Praeger, Westport.

Munro, A. (1995) *The Moons of Jupiter*, London, Vintage.

Munro, A. (1997) *Dance of the Happy Shades*, Toronto, Penguin.

Rasporich, B.J. (1990) *Dance of the Sexes: Art and Gender in the Fiction of Alice Munro*, Edmonton, University of Alberta Press.

Redekop, M. (1992) *Mothers and Other Clowns, The Stories of Alice Munro*, London, Routledge.

Thacker, R. (2011) *Alice Munro: Writing Her Lives: A Biography*, Toronto, McClelland & Stewart.

Ue, T. (2014) Incarceration, Focalization, and Narration: Adapting the Two Selves in *Boys and Girls*, *Short Fiction in Theory and Practice*, 4:2, pp. 175–185.

Ventura, H. (1992) Alice Munro's '*Boys and Girls*': Mapping out Boundaries, *Commonwealth Essays and Studies*, 15:1, pp. 80–87.

4 Extended Canadian Works

Lives of Girls and Women

By the Canadian director Ronald Wilson, *Lives of Girls and Women* was written by Charles K. Pitts and Kelly Rebar, with music composed by Lawrence Shragge. The producer was Richard Borchiver, with Raymond Massey and Jon Slan of Toronto's Paragon Entertainment as executive producers. Initially aired as a four-hour miniseries, the ninety-one-minute film was completed in 1994 and broadcast two years later on CBC television. Nominated for four Gemini awards, it won the 1995 Atlantic Film Festival. The actors included Tanya Allen (Del Jordan), Wendy Crewson (Ada Jordan), and Peter MacNeil (Tom Jordan). Shot in Pickering, Shelburne, and Toronto, *Lives of Girls and Women* is set in a suffocating rural Ontario in the 1940s: the town is Jubilee, but there are no precise temporal markers.

The credits acknowledge that the film is "based upon the novel by Alice Munro", referring to the writer's second work, *Lives of Girls and Women*, published in 1971. Unlike the film, the literary text provides a clear temporal reference, through the date the protagonist adds to a letter she is asked to write for Uncle Benny: "August 22, 1942" (Munro 2015, p. 15). The volume was promoted as a novel for editorial and marketing reasons: the author was under great pressure to write a novel, to provide proof of her writing skills, and to legitimise her status as a writer. Munro made strenuous efforts to master the novel form, through significant revisions in content and form, primarily to the last chapters (Thacker 2011, p. 211ff). However, the seven chapters and epilogue of *Lives of Girls and Women* would be better read as "interconnected short stories" or as "a short-story cycle". Interlinked yet independent chapters move the story forward from "The Flats Road", to "Heirs of the Living Body", "Princess Ida", "Age of Faith", "Changes and Ceremonies", "Lives

DOI: 10.4324/9781003183846-5

Figure 4.1 Becoming a writer. Lives of Girls and Women © 1996 photos used under permission from Octapixx Inc., Toronto, Canada. © 1996 photos used under permission from Octapixx Inc., Toronto, Canada.

of Girls and Women", "Baptizing", and finally, the "Epilogue: The Photographer". The main challenge faced by the script writers and the director was to achieve narrative cohesion while adapting a fragmented story; the issue is the main focus of this section.

The film appears to be a compact text, in a sequence of three distinct parts, each of about thirty-minute duration. Del (interpreted by a single actress) provides the *fil rouge* for the entire narrative, from the time she matures as a young woman in high-school, through her family tensions, spiritual and religious inquiries, as well as her sentimental and sexual experiences. Her personal development is made possible through her connections: with her mother in the first section, with her schoolmate Jeffrey and the radio host Mr. Chamberlain in the second, with her boyfriend Garnet in the third. The mother epitomises education, determination, self-affirmation, whereas Garnet introduces the themes of religion and passionate love. Less central characters Jeffrey and Mr. Chamberlain are functional to the development of Del's identity in relation to education and love. In what Leszczynska has defined as "the story of becoming an artist" (2016, p. 76), Del ultimately acknowledges her creativity and passion for writing (Figure 4.1). If the first and the third sections are the most important ones, the second operates as an in-between unit.

The film opens with the image of a young woman looking at her refracted image in the waters of a river. Holding her shoes in her left hand, she brings some water towards her face, accompanied by slow and melancholic instrumental music. A female adult voice-over can be heard: "Looking back I can see that the Wawanash river flew through my veins, but I didn't know it at the time and what I wrote then was not about my own world" (00:00:26–00:00:37). Through this introduction on the riverbank, the film suggests a high level of introspection and foregrounds the female character, the only human participant represented on screen at this point, as both narrator and focaliser. Further, it marks an important temporal distance between the narrated time and the time of narration and adapts what Howells in Munro's work calls "the double vision" (Howells 1998, p. 32). The time of events is described as a time when the protagonist lacked maturity, in both experience and awareness: Del confesses to being unaware of the relevance of the river to her identity and her writing. Reminiscent of *Connection*, the voice-over frames the narrative stance as a first-person homodiegetic narrator, even if the temporal gap between narration and narrative makes this definition unstable. Absent from the literary work, this opening section may be conceived as a Prologue, illuminating the film narrative in terms of character, setting, events, and perspective.

Del's Relationship with Her Mother

After the opening scene, the camera captures the charming figure of an adult woman, Ada Jordan, in a farm-house yard, who calls out: "Del!" A reverse shot shows the young woman running towards the adult woman and getting into a car. A second voice-over unit accompanies the images of the car moving across the dusty countryside: "The Flats Road was not part of town but it was not part of the country either. It was the last place my mother wanted to live" (00:01:40–00:02:00). The section introduces and develops the maternal figure and the conflictual relation she has with the place where she lives: the liminal Flats Road. A gregarious and ambitious woman, Ada needs a more dynamic environment where she can establish relationships and sell her encyclopaedias. When the car reaches an urban district, Del announces: "Jubilee!". This is where, hoping to transform her isolated lifestyle, Ada will rent a house with her daughter and son and take on a boarder, Fern. In this sequence, the voice-in is used twice in its naming function: first to name the protagonist (Del), then the town (Jubilee), providing the audience with clear interpretative tools for the fruition of the narrative.

The car stops in front of a humble house. Ada displays a volume of the encyclopaedia she is trying to sell, asking Del to recite the names of the US Presidents. After a moment of hesitation, Del obeys and lists the Presidents' names in front of an uncaring audience. On another occasion, Ada is hosted by Del's teacher and asked to present a competition to her class. The event, which entails an award for the best essay on the British Commonwealth, has been organised by the encyclopaedia company. The camera features Del's embarrassment, amidst her schoolmates' mocking gazes and laughs. However, Del's voice-over admits: "I couldn't help it: I shared my mother's appetite for knowledge" (00:02:39). If the visual track reveals Del's shame for her mother's assertiveness, the audio track confesses the protagonist's proximity to her mother's curiosity, intersemiotically framing Del's ambivalent feelings. A self-confident and curious person, Ada keeps raising intellectual questions, often in conflict with the surrounding environment. She writes letters to the local magazine editor and signs them with a nom de plume, *Princess Ida*, taken from Tennyson (00:06:20–00:06:32).

Like Margaret's mother in *Boys and Girls*, Ada is also a storyteller, who likes telling personal stories about her own youth, especially about how much she wanted to go to school, but had to do housework instead. Ada appreciates the daughter's prodigious memory but not her creative attitude. For this reason, Del decides to conceal her passion and hides the story she is writing. Unlike her mother, the young woman establishes an emotional and aesthetic connection with the place she inhabits, through physical observation, and makes it the core of her creative work. While walking back home from school, Del admires the leaves moving gently in the autumn breeze: "I took what I saw around me and found a way of nudging it into whatever story I was in the middle of" (00:04:53–00:05:27). The scene echoes the river scene and elaborates upon the value of the landscape for Del's writing. Cross-cutting leads the audience to her bedroom, indulging on her feelings, uncertainties, and frustrations towards the writing process. In a later scene set in Uncle Craig's office, Del closely admires her uncle's writing machine, which operates as a recurring visual metaphor across the whole film narrative that symbolises Del's aptitude for writing.

There Is a Change Coming

While further developing the depiction of the mother and the theme of Del's writing, the second section of the film revolves around other characters: her schoolmate Jerry, her best friend Naomi, her mother's boarder, Fern, and a frequent guest, Mr. Chamberlain. Scenes set at school offer insights into Del's social and political environment. Del and the most brilliant and promising student in her class, Jerry, are called to the board to draw a map of Ontario. Reference to provincial geography is of interest, especially in relation to the scenes from the previous section which marked the US Presidents and the British Commonwealth as relevant cultural systems. The exception in a film not overtly concerned with political issues, this unit frames the tension between local identity, the colonial legacy, and the cultural burden of the neighbouring USA. This issue will be elaborated upon later in the chapter.

Other scenes feature Del and Naomi talking about love, sex, and human anatomy. Having heard the local gossip about Fern, Naomi wants to know more. Del imagines a connection with a frequent visitor of the Jordan family, Mr. Chamberlain, the man who reads the news on the local radio. She asks her mother, who firmly rejects the daughter's insinuations; the spectator, yet, is invited to be cautious. During a family gathering, the newsreader furtively touches Del's breast, generating ambivalent feelings in the young woman. As the visual track shows, this harassment leads Del to attend to her physical appearance, sitting in in front of her mother's vanity table, trying out different hairstyles to see which is most attractive. Del's voice-over in the audio track, however, reveals her awareness that the man is trying to control and manipulate her, accusing her of being treacherous and provocative (00:41:00–00:41:15). One morning, Mr. Chamberlain picks Del up in front of her school and brings her to the riverbank, where he masturbates. In front of him, the young woman is "surprised and disbelieving" (Leszczynska 2015, p. 80). He also wants Del to intrude in Fern's room to look for some letters he had written, which she cannot find. Yet, she discovers the content of the letters through a confession of the boarder herself: Del and Ada find out about a past relationship between Mr. Chamberlain and Fern. A marriage had been promised but Fern had thereafter been abandoned. Later, Mr. Chamberlain leaves town, followed by Fern some days later: Ada loses a boarder and a friend.

Profoundly affected by Fern's story and departure, Ada talks to Del on the porch and utters the words that give the film its title, about a forthcoming change in the lives of girls and women.

There is a change coming, Del, in the lives of girls and women. But we've got to make it come. You know all we've had up till

Figure 4.2 "There is a change coming". Lives of Girls and Women © 1996 photos used under permission from Octapixx Inc., Toronto, Canada.

now has been our connection with men. All we've had. No more lives of our own, really, than domestic animals.

(00:49:03–00:49:21)

Ada advocates agency and responsibility for women (Figure 4.2). According to "the most forcible expression of the new order" (Beer 2009, p. 149), women cannot leave the power to plan and rule their lives to men. Left alone with her thoughts, Del interprets her mother's wish in a different direction. She plans to adopt a male code of behaviour: "Without even thinking about it, I decided to do what men did instead: go out and take all kinds of experiences" (00:50:24). Del's reaction is narrated in the third filmic section and encompasses sexual and aesthetic experiences.

The second section ends with Aunts Elspeth and Grace offering Del Uncle Craig's manuscript and his typewriter, asking her to finish the meticulous history of the region her Uncle had working on with devotion for years. The aunts explain that this gift should have been given to Del's brother, Owen, since he was a boy. The niece was however preferred, given her writing skills. When Del replies that she likes fiction, the two ladies are disappointed: to be a chronicler is much more prestigious in their eyes than to be a creative writer. Indeed, the interest Del has for this task is not of a scholarly nature: the archival work conducted by the uncle seems pointless to her.

However, as Leszczynska notes (2016, p. 79), "the inheritance of the typewriter is a milestone on the heroine's way to being a novelist".

Writing Things Down

The third section revolves around Del's "passionate affair" (Howells 1998, p. 45) with a new young man, Garnet. It starts during a religious ceremony Del attends out of curiosity: the young woman notices a boy who keeps looking at her. He then approaches, gently touches and holds her hand (00:59:10). Over the next days, he meets her in front of the school, asks for her address, and comes to pick her up so they can go to church together. In his truck, they talk about their lives and he tells her about his experiences in jail. Del is impressed by Garnet's profound knowledge of and contact with real life, while she perceives her own existence as ephemeral. In a dialogue with Ada in front of a mirror, Del laments: "I'm not in life. I just watch it" (00:36:05–00:36:08). Interestingly, the title of the adapted work by Munro was initially *Real Life* (Thacker 2011, p. 208).

Attracted by Garnet, Del follows him and leaves home when she should be studying for her exams to obtain a scholarship for university. Ada is disappointed: her daughter is wasting her time and concentration and may miss a unique opportunity for her future. The object of Ada's concern, Garnet is depicted by the camera as a self-centred person. One scene captures the young man gazing at Del in the side mirror of his pick-up, just in front of her house (00:73:43–00:73:45). Del is off-screen and spectators enjoy a close-up of Garnet's self-satisfied face as he watches Del in the side mirror. He has just convinced her to leave her books to follow him. This shot is reminiscent of a similar one in *Thanks for the Ride,* with George gazing at Lois in the rear-view mirror. By bringing a power unbalance into play, the intrusive, aggressive, male gaze expresses the privileged position of the gazer over the gazee. The day before her exams, Garnet brings Del home to meet his numerous and noisy family. On the porch of his house, under the roof, he carves Del's name at the end of the list of the names of his former girlfriends. This provides yet another symbol of male attempts to control and dominate Del. Garnet brings Del home very late and they have sexual intercourse in front of the wall. During the exam, Del's mind is absent, her thoughts devoted to her love relationship. As a result, she passes the exam without receiving a first-class mark, thus misses out on the scholarship.

This third section revolves around Garnet's attempts to control Del and the young woman's hesitation as she is torn between

Figure 4.3 Baptism. Lives of Girls and Women © 1996 photos used under
permission from Octapixx Inc., Toronto, Canada.

surrender in the name of romantic love and longing for her own
space. During an appointment, after having sex, Garnet mentions
his plans: their marriage, their future baby, her joining the Baptist
church. In a scene that evokes the beginning of the film, Del reaches
the Wawanash river and looks at the water surface. With her hand,
she scoops up some water and washes her face. Then she immerses
herself in the water, naked. After reaching her, Garnet tries to force
the young woman to be symbolically baptised (Figure 4.3): he holds
her under the water and nearly drowns her. In "a desperate struggle
for independence" (Howells 1998, p. 35), she liberates herself from
the young man's grasp and refuses the rite. After appearing in the
Prologue scene, the water flow appears again in topic scenes: it provides the setting for Mr. Chamberland's harassment and for Garnet's
failed baptism. The very site where Del is a victim of psychological
and physical male aggression is also the site of her rebirth. After the
film's climactic scene, Del walks back home, tears in her eyes.

On her way, she passes through a photographer's shop and her
voice-over reports her thoughts: "As I walked on to Jubilee, I repos-
sessed the world. Trees, houses, fences, streets jumped out of me as
if suddenly real, unconnected to the life of love. I felt my own self,
ironic, isolated, begin to breathe again" (01:26:14–01:26:49). Back
home, she circles some job announcements on the newspaper. Then
she starts using the writing machine she has inherited from Uncle
Craig and her voice-over reveals her thoughts:

> It did not occur to me that I would suddenly become so greedy
> of Jubilee. I had to, without delay, write things down. Lists. But

no list could hold what I wanted, for what I wanted was every last thing, every layer of speech and thought, stroke of light on bark or walls, every smell, pothole, pain, crack, delusion, held still and held together – radiant, everlasting.

(01:28:56–01:29:29)

Leszczynska (2016, p. 86) provocatively asks if it was real life which allows Del to write or if it is writing which allows her to find her real life.

Struggle for Cohesion

The film *Lives of Girls and Women* shows a high degree of intersemiotic consonance at the level of the *mise en scène*, narrative cohesion at the level of editing, as well as of contact with the adapted text. The film transfers the literary work to screen and the audience constantly finds echoes of Munro's text. Often quoting the adapted text, the voice-over pervades the cinematographic text to reveal Del's thoughts, feelings, and emotions. It frames Munro's "retrospective cast of the narrative style, which combines the insights of the mature writer with the adolescent subject" (Beer 2009, p. 144). Tension between the female protagonist and the narrative is aurally expressed, Leszczynska observes (2015, p. 15), in the voice quality difference between the voice-over ("deep and low") and the voice-in, which signals the temporal shift between the time of narrative and the time of narration. The use and function of the voice-over are similar to those in *Connection* but are ubiquitous throughout the film. Albeit more extended in duration, this film seems to adopt strategies seen in the short films released in the previous decade, such as the voice-over with its intratextual cohesive function and extensive connections with the adapted work.

From a compositional perspective, the film systemically seeks and achieves unity. In this pursuit, it omits the story of Uncle Benny, one of Munro's most beloved eccentric characters, around which the whole first chapter of the book revolves. It also cuts out the Epilogue intended as such (although some parts are anticipated in the main narrative) and compresses the parts about Uncle Craig. Overall, three distinct and separate sections are developed in the film narrative, each revolving around specific themes and motifs and focused on specific characters. Each section ends with a scene reflecting Del's writing experience, as a sort of refrain. To symbolically suggest Del's passion, the film relies indeed on Uncle Craig's typewriting machine, which is absent from the book. Evoking the car's role in *Thanks for the Ride*, this visual metaphor anchors her destiny. Its addition may be read as an attempt to assist text fruition, by foregrounding the main theme. The Prologue can be read in the same vein, since it clearly marks and signals the narrator's stance, the setting of the story, and the profile of the protagonist. Following are the main strategies of filmic cohesion:

- The pervasive voice-over;
- The omission of marginal characters;
- The foregrounding of the main characters;
- The addition of the Prologue;
- The repetition with variation of the river motif;
- The use of the typewriting machine.

Edge of Madness

This section discusses *Edge of Madness*, directed by the Canadian Anne Wheeler and written by Charles K. Pitts (who also co-authored *Lives of Girls and Women*) and Wheeler herself. Produced by Lions Gate Films, the film features Caroline Dhavernas as Annie, Brendan Fehr as Simon, Corey Sevier as George, and Tantoo Cardinal as Ruth. As intertitles state, the story unfolds in 1851, against the historical backdrop of Canada's pioneer past. The film is set in a region that would later become the Province of Manitoba, in Western Canada. The main setting is the Walley Gaol, administered by the Clerk of the Peace James Mullen: this is where the protagonist Annie is imprisoned, after confessing to the murder of her husband Simon. A second narrative line develops in a remote area of the Red River Valley (in a Scottish settlement for fur trade administered by the Hudson Bay Company) where Annie, Simon, and George lived before Simon's death (Bigot 2020, p. 43).

Edge of Madness opens as an exhausted and bruised young woman, Annie, reaches shelter at the Walley Gaol, having walked across the snow-covered wilderness. She claims she murdered her husband, but the Clerk of the Peace is sceptical and starts investigating what looks like a mysterious case: "In the absence of Governor Simpson, it's fallen to me to investigate this strange young woman who appeared last night" (00:04:54–00:05:10). The film's end provides a resolution: Simon's brother George confesses to the murder, which he committed to protect Annie from Simon's repeated physical and sexual abuse. However, Mullen decides not to denounce

George, who can thus marry Miss Treece, the daughter of some neighbours in the Red River Valley.

Revolving around the hard life of the pioneers, the film pervasively shows the violence committed against the female protagonist by her husband and the doctor. Indirectly, Wheeler also denounces the violence against the Métis, through labour exploitation, and against animals, through the fur trade (Bigot 2020, p. 44). The hard life she conducts and the violence inflicted on her lead Annie to the "Edge of Madness". The film progressively discloses what is behind an apparent condition of insanity. Numerous flashbacks unveil the woman's past: when Simon chose her from an orphanage, being in need of a wife (in a scene that, Bigot observes [2020, p. 42], evokes slave markets); when her husband regularly perpetrated violence upon her, while his brother tried to defend her; when she used to write letters to her friend Sadie. Only the memory of Sadie and the moments of happiness they shared at the Orphanage seem to console Annie. At the fort, support is provided by Ruth, an Aboriginal woman working for Mullen. With her caring and loving attitude towards Annie, Ruth understands that the young woman is pregnant. Ultimately, the spectator discovers that George is the father of the baby, named Sadie Herron. The end of the film is nevertheless positive and features a festive wedding party.

"A Wilderness Station" as Historiographic Metafiction

Wheeler's film is based on the epistolary narrative "A Wilderness Station", first published in April 1992 in the *New Yorker* and then, two years later, in Munro's eighth collection *Open Secrets*. Defined by Löschnigg as a "polyphonic story" (2017, p. 98), Munro's text is composed of eleven letters—the first dated January 1851, the last July 1959—and of one magazine article written by George Herron. All the documents have been retrieved by the historian Leopold Henry, from Queen's University. Henry is researching the life of the politician George Herron and, by implication, is drawing a picture of the nineteenth-century pioneer age in Southwestern Ontario (Duncan 2003, p. 99). Indeed, the short story unfolds in the Huron county, where two young brothers, George and Simon, settle in the middle of the bush with Simon's wife, Annie. After a while, Simon dies in an accident while clearing trees, but the different versions of the fact emerge across the letters, including one mentioning a murder. Eventually, Simon's death remains an unsolved mystery. Hence, Bigot defines (2020, p. 41) this short story as "enigmatic", as the architecture is built on "a series of documents that do not fit". Even scholars are not unanimous in their interpretation: Carrington (1996) argues that Annie's version is problematic, malicious, and unreliable, whereas Duncan sustains (2003, p. 101) that the woman should be trusted.

"A Wilderness Station" epitomises what Hutcheon (1988, p. 113) conceptualises as "historiographic metafiction", indicating self-reflective works on history, texts that primarily deal with history as discourse rather than with history as events. Historiographic metafiction denounces the constructedness of historiographic writing, of master narratives that legitimate, confirm, and perpet-uate entrenched dynamics of power and control. As a form of re-sistance, it promotes plural and contradictory accounts, unsolved conflicts, and open endings. In this vein, Munro unveils histori-cal writing shaped by those in power: Reverend Walter McBain, Mr. James Mullen, the Matron of the Orphanage, George Her-ron. The multi-perspectival nature of epistolary fiction is adopted to denounce the systemic commodification of the female subject. Annie is, indeed, the object of various master narratives projecting and confirming patriarchal, colonial, religious, and professional powers. These diverse stances define, label, and control the female subject, who remains voiceless for a long part of the story. Interest-ingly, in the short story, the protagonist's mind is defined as insane by both the doctor and the reverend. The medical authority identi-fies the reason as Annie's reading habits (Munro 1995, p. 205), while the religious authority points to her "not complete [...] submission to her husband" (Munro 1995, p. 203). Only later can readers hear Annie's voice.

Patterns of Adaptation

Munro has a passion for telling and retelling stories, and in "A Wil-derness Station" she engages both with her family past and with the literary genre, taking a creative, critical, and transformative ap-proach. Significantly, the kernel of the short story, Simon's death, is grounded on an authentic incident in Munro's paternal family history (Duncan 2003, p. 99). The author's great-great-grandfather was a Scots Presbyterian who left the Ettrick Valley in Scotland to migrate to Canada in 1818 (Carrington 1996, p. 71). Starting from authentic and tragic facts she learned from a memoir written by a cousin of the dead man, Munro inserts a female protagonist and describes the "hard, punishing pioneer life" (Duncan 2011, p. 62) of the Huron Tract from a gendered perspective. This family story is retold in a later text, "The Wilds of Morris Township", from the collection *The View from Castle Rock* (2006), which also incorporates fragments of the memoir.

The telling and retelling of stories in "A Wilderness Station" encompasses a tribute to her family and is also expressed through intertextual devices. Tellingly, among Munro's ancestors was James Hogg, nicknamed the Ettrick Shepherd, author of *The Private Memoirs and Confessions of a Justified Sinner* (1824). In his epistle to Mullen, Reverend McBain quotes this excerpt from the sermon "The Crook in the Lot" by Thomas Boston: "This world is a wilderness, in which we may indeed get our station changed, but the move will be out of one wilderness station unto another" (Munro 1995, p. 204). James Hogg knew Boston—who served as a minister in Ettrick from 1707 to 1732—and used his sermons in *A Justified Sinner* (Carrington 1996, p. 71). By mentioning the ceaseless afflictions human beings undergo, the intertextual fragment gives Munro's story its title and fulfils a multifaceted and multifunctional role. In the epistolary short story, "in addition to the literal wilderness of the setting and the metaphorical wilderness created by the story's narrative technique, the wilderness is a symbolic mirror of Annie's mind" (Carrington 1996, p. 72).

As Smith claims (2009, pp. 155, 156), the epistolary narrative engages with an established literary motif in Canadian writing, that of frontier literature, concerned with the depiction of the distant frontier past. Munro subverts the conventional lines of frontier literature, and, in line with Atwood, shows (1995, p. 159) that "it is not the wilderness that is fatal in [the] experience of a woman in the frontier". With a transformative approach towards the genre, the short story deconstructs the stereotyped depiction of the wilderness settlement as wild, dangerous, and violent. In the "reworking [...] of the tale of a colonial bride sent to a remote Ontario site in the mid-1800s", the story foregrounds "the unthinking objectification of the young woman as commodity" (Smith 2009, p. 159).

Closing in on Madness

Defined by Herz as "Munro's first proper film adaptation" (2013), Wheeler's *Edge of Madness* lasts ninety-five minutes. Differing from the story's title, which foregrounds the violence and dangers of the wilderness station, the film's title evokes Annie's psychological condition. The renamed screen adaptation thus shifts from exteriority to interiority. In many scenes, while writing to Sadie, Annie refers to the fact that she is going mad (e.g., 01:23:36–01:24:11). While questioning her refracted image in front of a mirror, she asks: "Am I wicked or insane?" (00:45:55–00:45:08). Annie's mental confusion is visually represented through a series of fragmented flashbacks: haunting images of fire. Mullen's voice-over reports on the questions his investigation has raised, connecting Annie's psychological condition to the life she led in the Red River Valley. He manages to outline "a picture of her life there: a hard life with a hard man. Hard enough to drive a woman to madness?" (01:13:47–01:14:22). Following Mullen, spectators are invited to raise and answer this question about the woman's insanity. They are offered two main tools: the close-up and the voice-over.

The main diegetic film line is composed of twenty-four sequences, unfolding from Annie's solitary walk in the snowstorm, to George's wedding ceremony and party. Most scenes are set in dark and claustrophobic Walley Gaol. The camera often captures Annie's movements, gestures, and actions, either when she is alone or while she is interacting or communicating with other characters. Across the various scenes, a privileged technique is the close-up of the young woman's face. This size of frame signals the woman as the main represented participant and her thoughts as the main mental processes. It also establishes an intimate social distance between spectators and the protagonist: Wheeler's pervasive and emphatic close-ups invite us to approach, observe, listen to, and feel with the female character. Through a multimodally shaped intimacy, spectators can therefore deconstruct the ideological label of madness attached to women in Southwestern Ontario's nineteenth-century pioneer past. In the filmic narrative, close-ups are often followed by fragments of Annie's memory and scenes from her past, outlining a second narrative line set in the Red River Valley wilderness. Close-ups, then, organise the film structure, acting as a cohesive device and linking present and past, actions and memories.

Triggered by the close-up, leaps into the past are often accompanied by Annie's voice. Her letters to Sadie are revealed through a voice-over operating as a sound bridge across shots: in the first letter Annie tells her friend how enthusiastic she is about her new married life, although her husband is taciturn (00:13:44–00:14:16). Yet, after the voice-over stops, scenes from the past show Simon's brutality as he physically and sexually abuses his wife. A further letter fragment gives voice to intimate and profound feelings "It was like being lost in the middle of the ocean. I felt so small" (00:20:46–00:21:02). Not only do these passages express her subjective perspective on events, they also reveal her cognitive and emotional approach to life, as well as her sensitivity. A later fragment shows Annie reading a passage from Robert Burn's pages, her voice-over reporting the text content (00:26:48–00:26:58). This aural device, together with the close-up, diminishes interpersonal distance and suggests reliability. In a later letter to Sadie, Annie describes her memories watching George drag Simon's corpse, since a falling tree had killed her husband. She also confesses the sense of relief she felt about her husband's death (00:54:18–00:56:25). This version, which spectators perceive as a reliable account, contradicts her initial confession as Simon's murderer. Progressively, the film shows that the woman is far from insane.

Accepting Wheeler's invitation, viewers appreciate this prismatic character and engage with Annie the mad, the reader, the seamstress, the adapter, the storyteller. In a constant story(re)telling process, the film acts as a site where previous stories intermingle, transform, and engender other stories. Generated by Munro's passion for storytelling and story(re)telling, Wheeler's film participates in the historiographic metafictional process and relies on different narrative modes and modal resources to retell Annie's story. The solution seems to intersemiotically translate, honour, and enhance Munro's project for her story: if the Canadian author aimed to include a female character in her story of the tragic family episode, the director places Annie at the ideational, interpersonal, and textual core of the audio-visual narrative.

Changes in the Film Adaptation

The issue of the fidelity is inappropriate for this adaptation, since various and profound lines of discontinuity seem to express an overt cultural and political project. As anticipated, a significant difference between the short story and the film is to be found in its ending: if the literary work leaves the mystery unsolved and the story open, the film achieves conflict resolution and narrative conclusion. In the film, not only does Mullen succeed in finding out who is responsible for Simon's death, but he also decides not to denounce the young man, having understood that his older brother Simon was violent and dangerous. Consistent with this resolution, the melodramatic tone pervading the happy ending and final resolution may be seen as balancing out the story's pervasive violence and hardness.

A second line of discontinuity between the book and film can be found in the function of the letters. In the short story, they provide a textual and epistemic mechanism for deconstructing the text and the truth: multiple authors express different positions, perspectives, and styles. The film, instead, alternates passages from Mullen's journal and passages from Annie's letters, thus contrasting the male authority and the female subaltern. The film, then, seems to unfold as a dual system: in terms of the settings, the temporal horizons, the perspectives on events. Both Mullen and Annie are often depicted in the process of writing: the content of their texts is revealed to the audience through the voice-over technique. However, when Annie's letter is returned because the addressee is deceived, Mullen decides not to inform the woman and to wait for further letters and further details. Thus, Annie's letters to Sadie are intercepted by Mullen, who can read the version of the story she confesses to her friend. In this way, he discovers George's responsibility in the murder. Letters in the film are used to uncover the truth.

As mentioned in the previous section, another line of divergence between the short story and the film regards the representation of the female protagonist. If the short story denounces her objectification through silencing and marginalisation by traditional history discourse, the film opens and closes with the female protagonist, first with her alone in the wilderness in the middle of a snowstorm, and then with her smiling face at George's wedding party. Annie is depicted not only while doing hard work but also while singing, dancing, and sewing. She is thus the main focaliser: spectators are offered her thoughts, her memories, her nightmares, triggered by the close-up and conveyed through the voice-over. Annie's centrality has implications for textual cohesion, one of the main challenges Munro's adapters have to face. While the adapted short story is fragmented and fractured, with neither frame narrator nor organising stance, the film achieves cohesion through Annie's pervasive and salient presence.

Notably, the change in setting is far from mere spatial dislocation. The short-story setting contextualises the narrative within Canada's colonial past, in the Huron County in today's Ontario. The film moves to the Red River Settlement in today's Manitoba. This relocation functions to support the account of the colonial tensions within the Canadian territory and within the Canadian pioneer culture. A symbolic place, Red River tells a conflicted Canadian story, since it is associated with the political figure of Louis Riel. The son of a French mother and a Métis father, Riel defended the rights of Métis minority groups against the recently established Canadian Confederation and was hanged for treason in 1885 (Hutcheon and Hutcheon 2020, p. 10). This change in setting, as well as the inclusion of the Aboriginal character Ruth, enables the Alberta director to articulate a political discourse within nineteenth-century Canada, by showing tensions between Eastern and Western Canada, between the minority groups and the anglophone power in the to-be Manitoba. Within the Canadian culture, Wheeler's film intertwines issues of gender and ethnicity, of power and hegemony. Specifically, dislocation frames an alternative perspective from where to observe and challenge Canadian society in light of nineteenth-century Canadian pioneer culture.

To sum up, this film adaptation engages with the adaptation process enacted by the Canadian laureate herself and by her protagonist. The adapted short story adapts a historical fact from a female perspective and quotes a Scottish sermon about a state of mind later emphasised in the film transposition. Tellingly, the protagonist of the adapted literary text, Annie, is a seamstress and a storyteller, who deftly adapts clothes and stories. It seems to me that *Edge of Madness* does not duplicate Munro's story but honours its adaptive approach and its gender concern. It develops its inclusive approach from a political perspective and within a historiographic metafictional frame.

Away from Her: Closeness and Distance

Away from Her (2006) by Sarah Polley is an extensively studied and much-admired adaptation, featuring Julie Christie as Fiona and Gordon Pinsent as Grant. Christie was awarded with the Best Actress Golden Globe and the Screen Actors Guild's Best Actress Award. The film received two Oscar nominations: one for Christie as female protagonist, one for Polley for her adapted screenplay. An actress, activist, and director, Polley is an iconic figure in Canadian culture, who was involved in the Canadian television series *Ramona* and *Road to Avonlea*. She also directed a six-hour episode of Atwood's *Alias Grace* and, in an interview given on the occasion of the Toronto Film Festival, she mentioned the long chats she had with the Canadian writer, who was given a cameo in the film. Unlike Atwood, Munro was "unreachable": when the young director received a voice message expressing film appreciation purportedly from Alice Munro, she thought it was a joke contrived by a friend.

The screen adaptation follows a seventy-year-old woman, Fiona, who develops Alzheimer's disease. When her symptoms become evident, Fiona is hospitalised in a clinic, where she establishes new social relations and falls in love with Audrey, another resident whose speaking and moving skills have been seriously impaired by a virus. After Audrey is released, Fiona suffers from a quick physical and mental decay. In order to relieve his wife's pain, Grant convinces Audrey's wife to bring the man back: when he reaches Meadowlake, Fiona shows a moment of awareness and recognises her husband again. Set in Ontario, in the late eighties or early nineties (Concilio 2018, p. 119), the film unfolds and intertwines three temporal levels: Fiona at Meadowlake, a recent past showing the symptoms of Alzheimer's, a more remote past resurfacing in the form of flashbacks (Berthin-Scaillet 2010, p. 170).

The film brought Munro's "The Bear Came over the Mountain", first published in the *New Yorker* and later anthologised in the collection *Hateship, Friendship, Courtship, Loveship, Marriage* (2001), to the screen. Defined by McGill (2016, p. 65) as "Alice Munro's most celebrated story", this text was later included in several selected-story collections and was republished by the *New Yorker* when Munro received the Nobel, thus considered as "*the* representative Munro text" (McGill 2016, p. 65). Critical attention to the story has been significant since its publication and has increased since the film's release.

For her short-story title, Munro borrows a line from a popular North American folksong. Based on repetitive patterns, the lyrics tell the story of a curious "bear that sets out on a quest to the other side of the mountain" (Herrera 2013, p. 112). Rather than extraordinary places and views, the animal only discovers the other side of the mountain:

> The bear went over the mountain, the bear went over the mountain, The bear went over the mountain, to see what he could see
> And all that he could see, and all that he could see
> Was the other side of the mountain, the other side of the mountain.
> The other side of the mountain was all that he could see.

At first, the bear may symbolically identify the male protagonist Grant, with his perceptive and cognitive limits in front of everyday life and its challenges. Observing "the opening up of expectations only to frustrate curiosity with the platitude of a tautological closure", Ventura (2010, p. 174) yet positions the intertextual reference within a tradition of Nonsense. Accordingly, the text would engender a tension between "the limits but also the redeeming possibilities of language" (Ventura 2010, p. 174). Munro, then, operates a minor (and, possibly, playful) adaptation of the song verse, changing the original verb "went" into "came", maybe suggesting interiority as the target for the bear's search.

The short-story title undergoes a significant renaming process from page to screen. The film title echoes a phrase from the story itself and expresses the reason why Grant accepted Fiona's marriage proposal: "He wanted never to be away from her. She had the sparkle of life" (2001, p. 276). Ventura observes (2018, p. 3) the sentimentality of a title evoking "the sense of a melodramatic parting", in sharp contrast to the detached tone of the story title. However, Ventura (2018) also notices a second reference in the short-story conclusion, when Fiona seems to recognise her husband in spite of her advanced stage of dementia: "You could have just driven away" she said; "Just driven away without a care in the world and forsook me. Forsooken me; Forsaken" (Munro 2001, p. 323). The wordplay around the verb forsake "seem[s] to assert the reparative dimension of language" and provides a more complex frame for title interpretation (Ventura 2018). The syntagm "away from her" is also present elsewhere in the short story, with reference to what Howells terms the "masquerade of faithfulness" (2009, p. 189), hiding Grant's infidelity during the 1960s and 1970s. The third-person narrator records that the Professor, in spite of his numerous affairs, "had never stopped making love to Fiona. He had not stayed away from her for a single night" (Munro 2001, p. 286). Thus, the clause chosen for the title occurs three times in the short story, with different connotations for the construction of the male character/focaliser and his relation with his wife. As the short-story title is only apparently childish, the film title is only apparently sentimental.

Beyond the Grant-Fiona relation, Herrera (2013, p. 110) reads the film metatextually and observes that the Canadian director uses specific cinematographic techniques to bring the audience "closer to her and *Away from Her*", "her" implying both character and author. On the one hand, proximity with the literary work is suggested as "nearly a third of the film's dialogue reproduces Munro's text almost verbatim" (Herrera 2013, p. 110). On the other hand, distance is expressed as Polley adds some scenes that "add more dramatic intensity to the condition of Fiona's disoriented mind" (Herrera 2013,

p. 108). More than this, in terms of content, some scenes are added, deleted, or modified; from a textual viewpoint, the film operates with processes of dislocation; from a socio-cultural viewpoint, the Canadian cultural background is expanded. In order to develop this argument, attention will be devoted to the representation of senile dementia, the characters of Fiona and Grant, and Canadian culture.

Fiona's Approach to Her Illness

Unlike the vague reference to a form of senile dementia in the literary text, the film explicitly names the illness Fiona is affected by (Berthin-Scaillet 2010, p. 159; Herrera 2013, p. 111). The camera shows the woman holding a volume devoted to Alzheimer's, its name clearly visible on the cover. Meanwhile, her voice-in reads passages from the book about the multiple challenges the caregiver of a patient affected by Alzheimer's disease has to face: "[The spouse] must put up with deranged, but at the same time very personal insults, and must somehow learn to smile through it all. The caregiver must diagnose a wide variety of ordinary ailments, under extraordinary circumstances". Reading from the volume continues for a while. After the initial scene where Fiona is on screen, the scientific text is read by her voice-over: sequential images show the kitchen, Grant, and the outside snow-covered landscape, with Fiona skiing (00:10:52–00:14:42). Later, after leaving Fiona at Meadowlake, Grant will read passages from the same medical volume, with the same voice-over technique upon landscape images: "Throughout much of the thinking brain, gooey plaques now crowd neurons from outside the cell membranes, and knotty tangles mangle microtubule transports from inside the cells" (00:41:45–00:42:56). The visual-verbal interface anchors the name of the disease and the voice-over-sound bridge signals its persistency.

Several cinematographic techniques express the woman's surprising awareness in front of the progressive regression of her cognitive skills. In a scene added by Polley, Fiona is missing the word "wine" during a dinner party (Berthin-Scaillet 2010, p. 167; Herrera 2013, p. 113). Captured in a medium shot, with a couple of family friends over a dinner table, Fiona stands up and takes a bottle in her hands to offer more wine to her guests. While the camera zooms on her face, she asks: "Would anyone like some more...?" and stops, unable to find the word she is looking for (00:08:30–00:09:25). The short story narrates, instead, Fiona's incapacity to cohesively utter the name: "Ice-land" (Munro 2001, p. 305), the country her mother came from. Signifiers progressively lose their sharpness, as well as the signifier-signified relation. The wine scene continues with an introspective unit showing Fiona's awareness, her voice-over confessing:

> Half the time I wander around looking for something which I know is pertinent. But then, I can't remember what I'm looking for ... once the idea is lost, everything is lost and I have to wander around trying to figure out what it was that was so important earlier.

On-scene again, Fiona adds: "I think I may be beginning to disappear" (00:09:30–00:10:08).

By observing illness representation, Concilio argues that *Away from her* depicts Fiona "as a woman of will and agency", with "strength and firmness of mind" (2018, pp. 104–105). Not a passive victim of the disease, she acquires information on her illness, elaborates upon what is happening, participates in the decisions to be made. When acknowledging her condition, she tells her husband: "We are at that stage, Grant, we are at that stage". He tries to minimise, but she is firm (00:18:00–00:19:10). She even provides comfort to the husband, unable to accept the situation: "You're not making this decision alone, Grant, I've already made up my mind" (00:19:40–00:20:28). Even later, he complains: "I don't think I like the place". And she answers: "I don't think we should be looking for something we like here Grant. I don't think we'll ever find that. I think all we can aspire to in this situation is a little bit of grace" (00:29:27–00:29:33). In a scene added by Polley and set at Meadowlake, she checks herself in autonomously and then sends Grant back home with a note (Keefer 2019, p. 34). While hospitalised, she helps, supports, and inspires Audrey. Concilio (2018, p. 104) sustains that the film confirms Munro's concern with providing agency to the old; both the short story and the film highlight the value of elderly people living together, providing mutual help and support.

Notably, the director celebrates Fiona's "playful awareness" (Concilio 2018, p. 112). In her script, Polley defines the woman as "ethereal, light, and sly. As though always enjoying a private joke" (2006, p. 3). She plays with her condition, with her husband, with words. After putting a frying pan in the fridge, Fiona tells Grant: "Don't worry darling. I expect I'm just losing my mind" (00:03:58–00:04:10). Before leaving her house to be admitted to the retirement home, Fiona looks at herself in an oval-shaped mirror in the entry-way and says "I guess I'll be dressed up all the time. Or semi dressed up. It'll be sort of like…". She puts on her coat, turns towards her husband, and completes the sentence with a touch of humour: "in a hotel". She then asks: "How do I look?" and Grant replies, "Just as you always looked", adding four adjectives taken from Munro: "Direct and vague, sweet and ironic" (00:30:04–00:30:54). This scene signals the woman's surprising ironic awareness, as she confronts her fate.

Fiona's privileged site for expressing her playful awareness is language. McGill notices (2016, p. 83) that Fiona is the one who "plays with language, renaming Meadowlake 'Shallowlake' and 'Shillylake' before settling on 'Sillylake'". The wordplay happens after getting lost in town and telling Grant: "You're going to have to put me in that place. Shallowlake?" (Munro 2001, p. 280). In the already mentioned story ending, she plays with the paradigm of the verb "forsake", "one of her old word jokes" (Howells 2009, p. 189). Epitomising her awareness of complexity (McGill 2016, p. 83), Fiona's creative and playful attitude towards language also evokes the adaptation of the title performed by the author herself, in the change from "went" to "came".

Grant as Husband, Caregiver, and Focaliser

Concilio (2018, p. 107) observes that *Away from Her* opens with Grant, who is holding an address written on a piece of paper: "Paris, Ontario" (00:23–00:42). He is driving towards Marian's house to ask her to bring Audrey back to Meadowlake, in an ultimate attempt to save Fiona, whose health condition has quickly deteriorated. The film opening has been significantly manipulated: moved from the position it holds in the literary text then fractured into smaller units and scattered across the first part of the film. This compositional strategy seems to depict Grant's bringing Audrey back to Meadowlake to relieve his wife's decay, as a signal of generosity. A sentimental interpretation is consistent with McGill's observation (2016, p. 84) that Polley's film does not overtly offer Grant's thoughts, through extended voice-over or added dialogue, which makes the film audience see him in a more sympathetic light. The same tempered connotation is achieved in the adaptation process through the obliteration of Grant's dreams (Berthin-Scaillet 2010, p. 169; Keefer 2019, p. 36).

The film's opening scene is followed by a flashback unit, in slow motion, evocative of an old celluloid (Berthin-Scaillet 2010, p. 158). Accompanied by Grant's voice and seen from Grant's point of view, the film shows a smiling eighteen-year-old Fiona looking straight at the camera. The voice-over reports that she proposed marriage to the young man and that he shouted yes; he never wanted to be away from her: she had the spark of life. Concilio observes that this scene is set in Port Stanley, Ontario, on the beach at Lake Erie (2018, p. 104). Then the image dissolves into white, accompanied by "Harvest Moon" by Neil Young (Keefer 2019, p. 40). This memory will reappear later, during Grant's conversation with the managing nurse Kristy about Fiona's state at the end of the film. In the short story, the fragment opens the narrative as a Prologue, whereas in the film it is represented as the projection of Grant's memory, told by his voice-over.

As such, Grant is the main and privileged focaliser in Munro's story, "with some commentary from an omniscient narrator" (Howells 2009, p. 187). As focaliser, however, Grant is presented in his perceptive and cognitive limits, rather than in his powers. The one not affected by dementia, Grant often does not remember episodes from the past, nor does he know the name of things (McGill 2016, p. 76). He does not remember the exact anatomic reason for Fiona's infertility, which was why they could not have children. He does not know many names for the furniture or appliances in Marian's house. He also avoids using the word "Alzheimer's" itself. McGill (2016, p. 75) interprets this refusal as a lack of awareness, not as the man himself claims, a disregard for labels: "it hardly mattered what label was put on it" (Munro 2001, p. 279). As a focaliser in the short story, the Professor of Old Nordic mythology and Icelandic skaldic poems is thus shown to be unreliable.

Throughout the film, the limits of Grant's perception and cognition are more nuanced. At the beginning, in the entryway mirror scene, his perspective is subtle and he is asked by Fiona to tell her how she looks. After mirroring herself, she asks him to act as a mirror for her (00:30:04–00:30:54). Later, the film adds a scene in which Grant admires himself in the mirror and smooths his hair in the entryway (00:45:02). The unit in the present triggers a memory, with Grant in his thirties in front of a bathroom mirror, smoothing his hair; a young Fiona behind him is encircling her arms around his waist and kissing his neck (Polley 2006, p. 49). If the film's beginning signalled his agency, these mirror scenes confirm Grant's role as the main focaliser in the audio-visual narrative and mark its introspective depth.

At the same time, the mirror scene reveals Grant's narcissism. Narcissus are the first flowers Grant brings to Fiona at Meadowlake, both on page and on screen, as noticed by McGill (2016, p. 71). When Grant enters the facility with the bouquet in hand, Kristy observes: "Wow. Narcissus this early" and adds with a patronising tone: "You must have spent a fortune" (Munro 2001, p. 292). In his "narcissistic tendencies", Grant even thinks that Fiona is making fun of him with her bizarre behaviour, "perhaps to punish him for his past infidelities" (McGill 2016, p. 71). In the film, the fact that "he makes her illness all about him" happens within a conversation with Kristy in more tempered terms. Grant in the short story projects a "limited, misogynist and self-interested perspective", whereas in the film is "gruff, wounded, charming and witty" (Newman 2019, p. 63).

Paradoxically, Grant's skills as focaliser are seriously impaired with Fiona's deterioration. In his intrusive search for his wife in the nursing home, he seems a "voyeur" (Howells 2009, p. 188). As Howells claims (2009, p. 189), "the nursing home starts to assume hallucinatory dimensions as Grant wanders around, getting lost in its labyrinthine passageways and always wondering if the different women he sees could be Fiona dressed up in somebody else's clothes", as if she were playing. Very often Grant looks for Fiona but wrongly believes he has spotted her or does not find her where he expects her to be. Inviting a woman-centred interpretation of Munro's story, Herrera (2013, p. 119) observes that Polley makes use of the technique of the "space-off", whereby a character, an object, a site is excluded from the frame. In the film, Fiona often enters the space-off, the ob-scene, thus symbolically leaving the perfect-wife position she has occupied throughout her life. In the last scene, Audrey will unexpectedly be in the film space-off.

Narrating Dementia: Onset, Development, Tricks

A "psychotic illness", Howells explains (2009, p. 187), Alzheimer's "fractures connections while in the process revealing the multiplicities of a self, obliterating some layers of recent memory and uncovering other forgotten layers hidden in the past". The short-story text surface seems less a cohesive entity than a collection of textual fragments. Fragments, however, are framed within an apparent temporal linearity: the short story starts with Fiona proposing Grant to get married and ends with her advanced stage of the disease. The film features numerous fragmented scenes, often regarding long-term memories of the past, but also showing scenes in the present. Examples of the former are the scene evoking of Fiona's proposal to Grant and scenes about Grant's extra-marital affairs resurfacing across the narrative. An example of the latter is the already mentioned second scene, where Grant is driving towards Marian's house. The film editing of this dismembered and fractured unit renders and enhances Munro's "disrupted and disruptive chronology" (Berthin-Scaillet 2010, p. 159). Paradoxically, the French scholar sustains, scene discontinuity and temporal shifts suggest the progression of the illness.

Alongside fractured connections, the discourse on dementia represents the development of the disease. Berthin-Scaillet argues that the film focuses on the progressive loss of memory and stresses that "[m]ost of the stylistic devices the film-maker resorts to are aimed at rendering a slow process of fading away" (2010, p. 159). At the textual level, rhythm is crucial in establishing this pace: slow motion pervades the narrative from the very inception of the narrative. The aforementioned second scene with Grant driving towards Marian's house is in slow motion. If this technique shapes the slow fading of memory at the intra-shot level, the dissolve fulfils the same semiotic function in terms of editing. From a logico-sematic viewpoint, Berthin-Scaillet (2010, p. 162) draws a connection between the dissolve and the blank space on Alice Munro's page. She considers, for example, the opening scenes devoted to Grant and Fiona practising cross-country skiing: they first move along parallel tracks in the snow-covered winter landscape, then they approach each other, leave each other, and again proceed together. If the mutual distance and interaction between the two on the snow symbolises their fluid relation in life, the fading of one shot into another "provides the choreography of the couple's life in common, on a filmic scale" (2010, p. 162). Herrera argues that Polley "resorts to the technique of dissolve to juxtapose episodes separated by distant time and space contexts, thus rendering a visual equivalent of Munro's narrative disruptions while framing the story in the subjective time of Fiona's mind" (2013, p. 109).

If cognitive and physical decay is formally expressed at the levels of rhythm and transition through slow motion and dissolve, Polley also resorts to some metaphors. At the visual level, Berthin-Scaillet (2010, p. 167) stresses the blurred image of the lit-up Christmas tree accompanying Fiona and Grant's dance the day before the departure to Meadowlake. Later in the film, their lit cottage is visible on screen but the lights then go out one after the other. Another scene shows Grant removing the Christmas lights on the front of the cottage (Berthin-Scaillet 2010, p. 167).

The way cognitive and physical decay slowly impacts everyday routine is represented through the pervasive stylistic device of repetition, which is also used as an editing technique. Berthin-Scaillet (2010, p. 163) highlights the obsessive repetition of the "long white corridor inside the retirement home". Grant, Fiona, and Audrey walk along the corridor eight times towards a dead end, shot by a camera which performs a minor zoom backwards and leaves them alone to experience and face the "gradual loss" implied by dementia. This pattern epitomises what Berthin-Scaillet (2010, p. 162) defines as "repetition stressing variation", or "inverted repetition". The French scholar draws on a subtle interpretation of this compositional pattern in connection with the extra-diegetic Bach's Prelude, whose tempo is divided into recurring series of eight notes, and whose sound stops when the camera along the corridor stops. The sound system intersemiotically reinforces the sense of abandonment expressed by the camera. Berthin-Scaillet (2010, p. 164) argues that the music of the film can be used as a clue to describe the whole process of adaptation performed by Polley:

> the intra-diegetic 'Prelude' by Bach is to be heard as part of a scene first, and is rewritten with a slightly different tempo and it is then used as the music of the film, which makes the original both recognizable and altered.

A similar effect of disconnection is achieved through the sound bridge and the cross-cutting. Berthin-Scaillet (2010, p. 160) provides the example of a cross-cutting centred on the two female characters of Marian and Fiona, who, in similar scenes, arrange flowers in their homes: purple in the case of Marian, yellow in the case of Fiona. The two scenes are divided by a cut but connected by the non-simultaneous diegetic sound of Grant's voice. By this compositional device of inverted repetition, Polley suggests the tension between the two women. Berthin-Scaillet (2010, p. 160) stresses the fact that Grant utters the term "before" both on-screen and off-screen, thus activating a previous memory in the present, as a form of remembrance of things past and of meaning-making in the present (with Marian) and past memory (with Fiona). Memories are not only unveiled and recovered but also reactivated and elaborated upon through editing techniques.

The story not only narrates the onset and development of the disease, but also its irregularity and nonlinearity. Like the literary narrative, the film narrative ends with a sudden and unexpected moment of awareness. When Grant brings Audrey back to Meadowlake to relieve his wife's pain, Fiona recognises the husband again and thanks him for his support. Polley writes in her screenplay (p. 108): "She lifts her arms to put them around him. He holds her, astonished. Settles into embrace. She pulls his earlobes. 'I'm happy to see you' She smiles, smells his shirt". The scene is accompanied by k.d. lang's version of "Helpless", achieving an effect of intersemiotic dissonance between the lyrics and the visual text. The final sequence continues with parallel tracks on the snow-covered Ontario landscape and ends with the image of young Fiona looking at the camera but, this time, turning her gaze away from the spectator (01:41:22–01:42:00).

The Canadian Culture

Ventura argues that: "the film is rooted in Canada, with Canadian flags sprouting up on-screen" (2018, p. 8), while Concilio sustains that it "shows its agenda of Canadianness" and that it can be considered "a Canadian cultural product" (2018, p. 107) through multiple traces. McGill (2008, p. 108) highlights that:

> [n]ot only does [Polley's film] retell a Canadian author's story without effacing its Canadian setting or local details, but it is also rife with national literary, cinematic, and musical intertexts, so much so that it effectively names its own Canadian artistic heritage.

The film, McGill observes, is rich in

> markers of Canadianness not found in Munro's text: references to Canadian Tire and the Ontario hamlet of Tobermory, Brant County road signs, a filing cabinet magnet with the national flag on it, and glimpses of a televised Toronto Maple Leafs game.
>
> (2008, p. 107)

Concomitantly, music is adopted to foreground the film's Canadianness (Concilio 2018, p. 116; Keefer 2019, p. 40; McGill 2008, p. 109). Two pivotal filmic moments are punctuated by music by the Canadian-born musician Neil Young. The first piece, "Harvest

Moon" with the refrain "Come a little bit closer, because I'm still in love with you", is used to accompany the dance by Grant and Fiona in their last day at the cottage before Fiona's hospitalisation. The music continues in the following scenes with a lower volume and stops when the couple reaches Meadowlake (00:29:43–00:30:10). The film's conclusion, with the previously described couple's hug in the sudden moment of awareness, is also accompanied by a song written by Neil Young: "Helpless," whose refrain represents Fiona's condition, "helpless, helpless, helpless, helpless". This scene is accompanied by the instrumental part, while the lyrics "There is a town in North Ontario" follow the snowing scene. However, this second song is performed by k.d. lang, an award-winning Canadian singer and political activist. Polley seems to celebrate Canadian adaptation culture alongside Canadian culture, especially from a gendered perspective.

Canadian writers are also present in the film. McGill notices (2008, p. 108) that Kristy reads from a copy of Alistair McCleod's *No Great Mischief.* A poem by Michael Ondaatje (the Anglo-Canadian author of *The English Patient*), "The Cinnamon Peeler's wife", is read by Grant to Fiona on the sofa, her head on his lap (00:03:47–00:04:35):

> You climbed the bank and said
> This is how you touch other women
> The grass cutter's wife, the lime
> Burner's daughter
> And you searched your arms
> For the missing perfume.

The verses, however, evoke the man's infidelity (McGill 2008, p. 107). It seems to me that, through these Canadian intertextual references, the film's sentimentalism becomes more nuanced than it appears.

Not surprisingly, the cultural heritage is affirmed in opposition to the US cultural system, in line with a consolidated Canadian tradition. McGill (2008, p. 108) and Keefer (2019, p. 40) point out a line from the script, uttered by Fiona, where the woman admits she and her husband do not watch films any longer: "all those multiplexes showing the same American garbage" (00:10:32–00:10:55). In the same vein, Keefer (2019, p. 40) highlights a passage "trenchantly" added by Sarah Polley, where Fiona, Grant, and other residents watch the TV news at Meadowlake. Fiona's face and body are visibly marked by the disease. The journalist reports on: "the men and women of the United States armed forces, now overseas as the police of a troubled world" while showing violent images of the 2003 Iraq invasion, with air strikes against Iraqi people. "How could they forget Vietnam?", asks Fiona, whose senile dementia makes her words sound more powerful. Polley's script writes that "This sounds very much like her as she was" (2006, p. 80). Overall, the Canadian adaptation industry may be inscribed within a broader system of cultural promotion, based on visibility and celebration of Canadian texts. In other words, McGill (2008, p. 110) "speaks to the significance of adaptation for a country in which many artists and critics have been preoccupied with building a sense of a national cultural heritage". By this, Polley seems to embrace the cultural project developed by the CBC with earlier films, in a more independent and creative way.

Overall, the two narratives significantly differ in tone. Berthin-Scaillet (2010, p. 170) denounces a filmic "overstatement" as the couple parts for Fiona's admission to the clinic. This occurs in a "melodramatic" dialogue, in which Fiona asks: "Please don't go away from me like this". The effect is that of "an excess of pathos" (Berthin-Scaillet 2010, p. 170). In the same vein, Newman writes of a "romanticised final scene" with Fiona's unexpected recognition of the husband (2019, p. 59). He generally finds the film is "elegiac", while the literary text is "tonally and morally more ambiguous" (Newman 2019, p. 59). However, Munro's style is inherently very detached and vague: criticism of Munro has unanimously stressed her indeterminacy and elusiveness (Duncan 2011). Then, the audiovisual medium is per se more explicit than the literary text, as images inevitably show what words can evoke and suggest in a more oblique way. Polley's aesthetic and cultural choices are different in a consistent way: the film is explicit in naming and describing the disease, in portraying the Canadian context and culture, in representing Fiona's complex character. As such, the sentimental side of Fiona's character seems to express her prismatic identity. It may be associated with several other facets, including her acute irony (about her illness but also towards Grant), her critical perspective (in the scene about Vietnam war), her profound compassion (for instance with Aubrey). Polley succeeds in rendering Fiona as not only vague and sweet but "direct and vague, sweet and ironic", succeeds in showing her "sparkle of life".

References

Atwood, M. (1995) *Strange Things: The Malevolent North in Canadian Literature*, Oxford, Clarendon Press.

Beer, J. (2009) Short Fiction with Attitude: The Lives of Boys and Men in the Lives of Girls and Women, in H. Bloom (ed.) *Alice Munro*, New York, Bloom's Literary Criticism, pp. 143–152.

Berthin-Scaillet, A. (2010) A Reading of *Away from Her*, Sarah Polley's Adaptation of Alice Munro's Short Story *The Bear Came Over the Mountain*, *The Journal of the Short Story in English*, 55, pp. 157–171.

Bigot, C. (2020) Alice Munro's *A Wilderness Station* and Anne Wheeler's *Edge of Madness:* Filling in the Blanks, in S. Francesconi, G. Acerenza (eds.) *Adaptations of Stories and Stories of Adaptation*, Trento, Trento UP, pp. 37–55.

Carrington, I. de P. (1996) Double-Talking Devils: Alice Munro's *A Wilderness Station*, *Essays on Canadian Writing*, 58, pp. 71–92.

Concilio, C. (2018) The Mark on the Floor. Alice Munro on Ageing and Alzheimer's Disease in *The Bear Came over the Mountain* and Sarah Polley's *Away from Her*, in C. Concilio (ed.) *Imagining Ageing, Representations of Age and Ageing in Anglophone Literatures*, Bielefeld, Transcript Verlag, pp. 101–125.

Duncan, I. (2003) Persuasive Testimony in Alice Munro's *A Wilderness Station*, *Studies in Canadian Literature*, 28:2, pp. 98–110.

Duncan, I. (2011) *Alice Munro's Narrative Art*, London, Palgrave Macmillan.

Herrera, J.R. (2013) Away from Her? Sarah Polley's Screen Adaptation of Alice Munro's *The Bear Came Over the Mountain*, *Brno Studies in English*, 39:2, pp. 107–121.

Howells, C.A. (1998) *Alice Munro*, Manchester, Manchester UP.

Howells, C.A. (2009) Intimate Dislocations: Alice Munro, *Hateship, Friendship, Courtship, Loveship, Marriage*, in H. Bloom (ed.) *Alice Munro*, op. cit., pp. 167–192.

Hutcheon, L. (1988) *A Poetics of Postmodernism: History, Theory, Fiction*, London and New York, Routledge.

Hutcheon, L., Hutcheon, M. (2020) Adapting His Story: Louis Riel in History, Drama, Opera, and Staging(s), in S. Francesconi, G., Acerenza (eds.) *Adaptations of Stories and Stories of Adaptation*, op. cit., pp. 3–19.

Keefer, J. (2019) A Tale of Two Adaptations: Sarah Polley and Pedro Almodóvar do Alice Munro, in J. Novaković, V. Lopičić (eds.) *Canada 150 Filmed*, Belgrade, University of Belgrade Press, pp. 31–52.

Leszczynska, E. (2015) *Time, Space and Events in* Lives of Girls and Women: *An Analysis of the Short Story Circle by Alice Munro and Its Film Adaptation*, unpublished MA dissertation.

Leszczynska, E. (2016) Del Jordan: Becoming a Writer, in M. Buchholtz (ed.) *Alice Munro, Understanding, Adapting, Teaching*, op. cit., pp. 75–87.

Löschnigg, M. (2017) Carried Away by Letters: Alice Munro and the Epistolary Mode, in J. Fiamengo and G. Lynch (eds.) *Alice Munro's Miraculous Art: Critical Essays*, Ottawa, Ottawa U.P., pp. 97–113.

McGill, R. (2016) Mistaken Identities in *The Bear Came over the Mountain*, in R. Thacker (ed.) *Alice Munro*, London, Bloomsbury, pp. 65–85.

Munro, A. (1995) *Open Secrets*, London, Vintage.

Munro, A. (2015) *Lives of Girls and Women*, London, Vintage.

Newman, D.A. (2019) From 'Flowery Expression to Floral Motif: Adapting Discordant Narration in Sarah Polley's Away from Her, *Ekphrasis*, 2, pp. 54–72.

Polley, S. (2006) *Away from Her*. Script.

Smith, R. (2009) Rewriting the Frontier: Wilderness and Social Code in the Fiction of Alice Munro, in H. Bloom (ed.) *Alice Munro*, op. cit., pp. 153–165.

Thacker, R. (2011) *Alice Munro: Writing Her Lives: A Biography*, Toronto, McClelland & Stewart.

Ventura, H. (2010) The Skald and the Goddess: Reading "The Bear Came Over the Mountain" by Alice Munro, *The Journal of the Short Story in English*, 55, pp. 173–185.

Ventura, H. (2018) The Scandal of Misprison: Alice Munro on Screen. "The Bear Came over the Mountain" and *Away from Her, Between*, 8:16, htttp://betweenjournal.it

5 International Screen Adaptations

Bending Fate in *Hateship Loveship*

Hateship Loveship, released in 2013, was directed by the American director Liza Johnson, with a screenplay by novelist and short-story writer Mark Jude Poirier and music by Dickon Hincliffe. Actors include Kristen Wiig as Johanna Parry, Guy Pearce as Ken, Hailee Steinfeld as Sabitha, and Nick Nolte as Mr. McCauley. The plot revolves around the "unexceptional life" (Chang 2013) of Johanna Parry from Plainfield, a caregiver and housekeeper at the service of Mr. McCauley and his granddaughter Sabitha. The teenager lives with the grandfather, since her mother Marcelle had died many years before in a car accident caused by her drunken husband. Sabitha's father, Ken, lives in Chicago and is busy with a motel project he wants his sceptical father-in-law to invest money in. The narrative kernel focuses on an epistolary exchange between Ken and Johanna that is intercepted by Sabitha and her friend Edith, generating a faked correspondence. What starts as a game played by two school girls has radical effects for the adult people involved, and profoundly mutates their lives (Schuh 2014, p. 63). In fact, Johanna eventually moves to Chicago, marries Ken, and they have a child.

The film adapts the short story "Hateship, Friendship, Courtship, Loveship, Marriage" from the 2001 collection with the same title. Probably influenced by market constraints, the film changes this name in length and structure, offering a shorter and simpler version, based on a dichotomic logical pattern: *Hateship Loveship*. However, reference to the original title is preserved in a scene when the two teenage girls are drinking alcohol in Sabitha's room and playing a game proposed by Sabitha. The girl takes her name and that of the desired lover, Stephen, removes duplicated letters, and then counts "Hateship, Friendship, Courtship, Loveship, Marriage" on her

DOI: 10.4324/9781003183846-6

fingers for the number of unlike letters, to predict what kind of relationship the couple will have. Sabitha comments on the result she obtains, "friendship": "the only thing worse than friendship is hateship" (00:17:58–00:18:20). The filmic unit both quotes and engages with Munro's adapted title, outlining "traditional female destiny" as its frame (Howells 2009, p. 176). Hence, the scene is significantly positioned after Ken's first and only real written note to Johanna and before Johanna's answer, when everything is possible and when the girls decide to actively intervene in the correspondence. Symbolically, this seemingly ephemeral game operates as a diegetic trigger, anticipating the girls' wish to bend fate through romantic fantasy. It also hints at the possible impact of the forged correspondence, challenging the border between romantic imagination and real life (Bodal and Stehlau 2016).

Munro's story is set in Canada, between rural Ontario—where McCauley and Sabitha live—and Gydnia, Saskatchewan, Ken's residence. Ken and Johanna will finally move to Salmon Arm, in British Columbia, echoing regular movements across Canada in Munro's life and *oeuvre*. Within the pages, numerous references are made to Canadian territories. For example, the ticket agent at the train station provides Johanna with accurate instructions on her journey to the Canadian West:

> Wait in Sudbury for the Montreal train, but you won't get off there, they'll just shunt you around and hitch on the Montreal cars. Then on to Port Arthur and then to Kenora. You don't get off till Regina, and there you have to get off and catch the branch-line train.
>
> (Munro 2002, p. 5)

In contrast, Johnson's *Hateship Loveship* was filmed in New Orleans, LA, although exact locations remain undefined on the screen. Julyth Keefer observes (2019, p. 40) that:

> Johnson shifts the story's settings from Ontario to the American Midwest [Iowa], and from the Saskatchewan prairies to Chicago [where Ken lives]. A few stars and stripes are thrown into the *mise en scène* to identify the action as *echt* American, though not exactly Hollywood.

Similarly, the temporal background does not correspond in the two texts: the short story is set in the 1950s, whereas the film is set some decades later, as the presence of iPhones demonstrates. However, precise temporal markers are missing in both works.

Ankle Socks and Robust Shoes: Johanna

The opening cinematographic scene features an old woman who is about to die. In a final wish, she asks her committed caregiver Johanna if she can wear her blue dress. Johanna fulfils the woman's request with competence and empathy and, after her death, prepares the body for the funeral. The *mise en scène* shapes an intimate and respectful atmosphere: the exterior sunlight is filtered by the curtains and no musical accompaniment can be heard (00:00:00–00:03:34). If the sequence finds no equivalent in the short story, the spectators can retrieve some patterns from the story itself, since the film partially extracts the content of a real letter by Johanna to Ken positioned in the middle of Munro's text. In that epistle, Johanna writes that she spent twelve years with Mrs. Willets in Mourning Dove Dale in Northern Ontario, until the woman's death aged ninety-six. The dislocated filmic introduction outlines the psychological and emotional portrait of the protagonist, who is depicted as a caring and committed person. As a result of size of frame and angle, the audience immediately establishes a close interpersonal connection with Johanna. In terms of composition, the opening sequence also enables the film to start at a chronologically earlier period of time, when Johanna worked as a caregiver before moving to McCauley's house. Evoking similar solutions in earlier film adaptations, such as *Lives of Girls and Women*, this narrative strategy provides a Prologue and Premise that both orient and sustain fruition of the film narrative.

If the film foregrounds and celebrates a connection with the protagonist through this change in composition, the short story adopts a slow and indirect approach. As a matter of fact, Munro's short story opens *in medias res*, at the train station, where Johanna is buying a ticket to send furniture to Saskatchewan. Readers are offered the ticket agent's perspective upon the female protagonist, and focus on "a high, freckled forehead and a frizz of reddish hair" and teeth "crowded to the front of her mouth as if they were ready for an argument" (Munro 2002, p. 3). Wondering about her age—possibly under forty—, the agent concludes: "No beauty queen, ever" (Munro 2002, p. 4). A blank space introduces a section devoted to the man's thoughts upon Johanna. Unknown to him and not related to anyone that he knows in town, the woman does not wear a ring on her left hand. Unsurprisingly, she is not married. She looks like a farm woman ("shoes, and ankle socks instead of stockings, and no hat or gloves in the afternoon" (Munro 2002, p. 7)), but her manners and her self-confidence reveal something different. A further viewpoint on Johanna is offered, later in the story, by McCauley, who denounces Johanna after she leaves his house with the furniture. However, he is unable to describe her to the ticket agent: "He could not think how to describe Johanna—was she old or young-looking? thin or moderately heavy? what was the color of her coat?" (Munro 2002, p. 19). Notably, the reader's attention is drawn towards Johanna by the perceptive and cognitive limits of the two male focalisers (evoking Grant in *Away from Her*). Nourished by morbid curiosity, the station master's lens provides a biased and unreliable filter. McCauley's focalisation is, instead, defined by his cognitive incapacity to describe Johanna. In the literary text, the negotiation of distance is fluid, also enhanced by multiple focalisations. Differently, the opening scene of the film (with Johanna as the emphatic caregiver) immediately shapes an intimate connection between the spectators and the female protagonist, which remains stable throughout the whole narrative.

In line with the literary portrait, Johanna is at the same time fragile and strong, innocent and stubborn. She wears weird clothes, ankle socks, robust shoes. She always has a flowered apron on when she cleans, cooks, or irons (which is how she spends most of her time). The target of a forged correspondence, Johanna is also the one who invents a wedding when buying a new dress, announcing to the saleswoman: "It's probably what I'm gonna be married in" (00:33:34–00:35:52). The victim of fake/fictional writing, the protagonist is a storyteller herself. In the story by Munro, she decides to be reticent about the correspondence and not to mention it to Ken when they meet: "[it] might be better never to mention the letters in which he had laid himself open to her" (Munro 2002, p. 52). By virtue of this silence, the epistolary exchange is acknowledged and foregrounded. In the film, the faked letters are instead explicitly mentioned by Johanna, who asks twice about them. In response, Ken admits to not having received any e-mails and not even having a computer (00:46:22–00:47:02). Later, Johanna and Ken often comment on the teenage girls forging their letters, showing awareness of and distance from what has happened. If the literary text leaves ambiguities and contradictions untold and unresolved, the film ends with clarification and resolution.

This direct approach is consistent with a more general trend in the film's script: the on-screen characters are less prismatic than the ones on the page. In the literary text, McCauley's daughter, for instance, had been a turbulent young woman, whereas in the film, she is only an innocent victim of the husband: her death was due to the man's drunken driving. In turn, Ken is an unreliable profiteer who wants the sceptical father-in-law to finance his motel project. In the story, his counterpart is more nuanced: he had served in the army and sends letters to his daughter. Following the same logic enacted by the renamed title, the filmic characters are polarised, with McCauley and Marcelle becoming Ken's victims. Within this black-and-white system, Johanna's positivity is not only foregrounded but established at the very beginning of the film narrative and consistently developed across the scenes (Scott 2014).

Writing Letters as Writing Life

Alongside composition and character depiction, the divergent use of the letters in the two narratives is of interest. The short story by Munro is an epistolary work and letters are the short-story protagonists. First, epistles convey information about characters, events, and places. Second, letters establish social relationships among characters and between the narrator and reader: all texts written by Johanna show her devotion to others, be they McCauley, Sabitha, or Ken. Letters, finally, configure a fractured and layered textuality.

The film offers a distinct treatment of the letters in terms of presence, distribution, remediation, and transcodification. Johnson updates and "remediates" (Bolter/Grusin 2009) the letter correspondence by using, instead, an e-mail exchange. In her first faked letter, Edith suggests avoiding paper correspondence to save time and money (actually, to avoid her handwriting being recognised). In the film, the appearance of letters is rather faithful to the literary text, except for the absence of the first letter in the film and the reduction in the number of letters from Ken to Sabitha. More significant divergences are evident in terms of the distribution of the literary and cinematographic texts. Munro's short story includes eight letters, distributed across three out of fourteen sections. The correspondence is thus given a relatively central position, whereas in the film, it is brought forward. From a narrative viewpoint, it thus operates as the narrative kernel in the literary text, but as a premise in the film. This seems to suggest that Munro foregrounds the relevance of letters per se, whereas Johnson focuses on what they allow to happen, that is, their instrumental value. This impact evokes the letters intercepted in *Edge of Madness*, which enabled Mullen to solve the mystery of Simon's death.

Seemingly unproblematic, the adaptation process foregrounds a tension between the letter as text and the correspondence as process. The short story is focused on the epistles as textual fragments, explicitly displayed, embedded within the narrative in between blank spaces, whereas the film indulges in the process of correspondence, depicting Johanna while reading, writing, and waiting for letters. The first real note by Ken is given by Sabitha to Johanna. The camera shows the verbal text to the audience, who thus enjoy Johanna's angle and can read alongside her. It then becomes less intrusive and moves back, to let Johanna sit down on her bed and answer the thank-you note (00:16:48–00:17:57). When the housekeeper asks Sabitha for her father's address, Edith offers to send the card for her at the post office (00:18:42–00:20:18). At school, Edith opens the envelope and starts reading the letter, with frequent comments on formal inaccuracies or on stylistic ingenuity. The young woman writes the answer on the computer: she composes the letter aloud with Sabitha, who offers some suggestions but remains backgrounded in the *mise en scène* (00:20:19–00:23:02). It is through Edith's voice-in that spectators know of the content of these letters, which foregrounds her role and responsibility in the "malicious game" (Howells 2009, p. 177). The film ends with the graduation ceremony, where Sabitha and Edith are celebrated for their educational achievements. The concluding dialogue is again between Edith and Johanna. Edith asks the woman who is staring at her: "What do you want?" and Johanna answers in a self-confident way: "I have what I want". In what seems Johanna's affirmation, the young woman is ultimately left speechless.

Munro's text devotes attention to a multi-perspectival description of Sabitha's friend. In a passage reporting Johanna's thoughts, Edith is described as "smart" but as having a bad influence on Sabitha, as making her "sly" (Munro 2002, p. 17). Towards the conclusion, Johanna refers to Edith as Sabitha's "shifty friend" (Munro 2002, p. 52). Edith's father accuses his daughter of being "sarcastic", after a meeting with McCauley (Munro 2002, p. 27). The third-person narrator reports that, after Sabitha's departure, Edith

> had reverted to being the person she had been before Sabitha came along. 'Old for her age', diligent, critical. [...] She believed that her cleverness was going to be recognized and acclaimed

and an important future would open up for her. The past year's
silliness with Sabitha was slipping out of sight.

(Munro 2001, p. 28)

Yet, the sense of guilt for what she had done to Johanna made her
feel "a chill from her past, an invasive alarm. She tried to bang a lid
down on that, but it wouldn't stay" (Munro 2002, p. 28). Readers
are informed of her prodigious memory (a detail which suggests
the connection with the author herself). Unsurprisingly then, the
short story closes, with Edith working on a Latin translation at the
kitchen table, after discovering the existence of Omar, Johanna's
son. She renders Horace's passage, "Tu ne quaesieris, scire nefas,
quem mihi, quem tibi" into English: "You must not ask, it is for-
bidden for us to know [...] what fate has in store for me, or for you"
(Munro 2002, p. 54). Unlike the film's definitive conclusion, this focus on Edith and the Latin passage challenges our control of the
destiny and of the story.

To conclude, several lines of engagement can be seen in the
adaptation:

- A temporal gap between the adapted narrative and the adaptation is shaped.
- The correspondence is foregrounded as a process and as a
  diegetic element.
- An opening sequence is added.
- An intimate social distance between spectators and the protagonist is established and constantly maintained.
- Through chronological linearity in the narrative development,
  a fluid fruition of the story is sustained.
- Sabitha and Edith's educational achievement and Johanna's
  personal fulfilment conclude the film.

Overall, if the literary work fractures textual unity, challenges
readers, and resists closure, the film develops a linear, fluid, and
conclusive narrative.

Juliet Travelling to Spain

This section concentrates on the screen adaptation of "Chance",
"Soon", "Silence" from the collection *Runaway*. The three short stories were first published, exceptionally together, in the *New Yorker*,

between 14th and 21st June, 2004. Variously defined as a "trilogy", a "trio", a "tryptic", a "three-story cycle" (Thacker 2011, p. 515ff), the texts are closely intertwined, as they follow the life of a single female character, Juliet. In "Chance", readers meet Juliet in her early twenties. She is working on her Ph.D. in classics and has accepted a temporary teaching position in a private school in Vancouver. She surprisingly receives a letter from Eric, a fisherman she had met six months before on a Toronto-Vancouver train ride. When the young woman decides to visit Eric where he lives North of Vancouver, she discovers that his invalid wife has just died. "Soon" narrates the story of Juliet living with the fisherman and their baby Penelope in North Bay. Juliet visits her parents in the small town near Toronto where she has grown up so they can meet the child. During the stay, Juliet faces the pervasive narrow mindedness of her home village. She also discovers that her mother's health is frail; soon this will lead to her death. "Silence" revolves around Juliet as a middle-aged woman, working as a television presenter. She is alone: Eric died during a violent storm while fishing at sea; Penelope left her to join a spiritual community. Desperately but in vain does Juliet try to communicate with her daughter.

Almodóvar's Story of Adaptation(s)

Juliet's stories were turned by Pedro Almodóvar into a film, *Julieta*, shot in Spain and filmed in Spanish. Produced by the Warner Bros, Julieta was presented at the 2016 Cannes film festival, where it competed for the Palme d'or. Actors include Adriana Uguarte and Emma Suarez as Julieta, Daniel Grao as Xoan, Priscilla Delgrado and Blanca Parés as Antìia. The original soundtrack is by Alberto Iglesias while the screenplay is by Almodóvar himself. The Spanish director has a solid international reputation and, among his numerous films, several are adaptations of literary works. As Keefer observes (2019, p. 41):

> Almodóvar has often taken on, however promiscuously, literary adaptations: Cocteau's *La Voix Humaine* informed *Women on the Verge of a Nervous Breakdow*n, Ruth Rendall's *Live Fles*h became his *Live Fles*h and Thierry Jonquet's novel *Mygale* inspired *The Skin I Live in:* during the latter's opening moments a Spanish translation of Munro's *Runaway* appears for a tantalizing moment.

Expressing an appreciation for the Canadian writer's work, this cinematographic announcement inscribes *Julieta's* project within the Spanish director's personal "story of adaptation(s)" and creates intertextual connections within his individual film production.

In several interviews, Almodóvar gives voice to his reaction and relationship to Munro's stories (Bradshaw 2016; Kermode 2016). He defines his work as a tribute to the Canadian author, quoted as a direct source in the credits. Albeit acknowledging the greatness of the narrative and the depth of introspection, he admits he could not adapt the story without actively engaging with the narration. For example, when he first read the Trilogy, he found Juliet's approach to the mother during her visit to her hometown unbearably cold and detached (Bradshaw 2016; Kermode 2016). In turn, cinematographic reviewers familiar with Almodóvar's style foreground a discontinuity with the director's previous works, as he leaves melodrama aside and seeks a more austere tone (Romney 2016). The stylistic conflict and tonal concern are epitomised in the story of the film's title: the choice was determined by distribution constraints rather than by aesthetic logics. Indeed, the title the director initially had in mind, *Silence*, was changed because a film with the same title by Martin Scorsese was to be released in the same period. The original choice, however, reveals a slightly different perspective, since "Silence" is the title of the third and final story by Munro and foregrounds the punishment perpetrated upon the protagonist by the daughter. Placing emphasis on the female protagonist's relevance for the narrative, the new title gives agency to Julieta and suggests the director's transformation of the Trilogy as a unique and cohesive story.

Julieta's Letter-Writing Scenes

Evoking a compositional strategy adopted in *Away from Her*, the whole film architecture is anchored in the last story by Munro, "Silence". An adult woman, Julieta lives in a spacious and modern apartment in Madrid. Abandoned by Antiia without a word of explanation, she is overwhelmed by the grief and silence her daughter has left behind. A self-portrait by the British painter Lucian Freud hanging on the white wall of Julieta's aseptic house operates as the "objective correlative of Julieta's emotional ruin" (Keefer 2019, p. 48). The Canadian scholar observes that Julieta is a flat character, "capable only of guilty self-sacrifice and sorrow" (2019, p. 50) and writes of the director's "reduction of Julieta to a disempowered *mater dolorosa* in the course of the film" (2019, p. 50). Ignjatović (2019, p. 61) even considers Julieta to be a "martyr", unable to elaborate upon the early loss of Xoan and the later loss of Antiia.

A chance encounter between Julieta and Antiia's friend Beatriz allows Julieta to discover that the two met on lake Como and that her daughter lives in Switzerland, a mother of three. This unexpected piece of news has a profound emotional impact on Julieta, who abandons her plans to move to Portugal with her partner Lorenzo. Instead, she rents a flat in the same building where she used to live with her daughter, and starts writing a report on what she has discovered (00:10:00ff). The file slowly develops into a letter to her daughter read by her voice-over. In the epistle to Antiia, Juliet tells the story of how she first met her father Xoan on a train, how she received a letter from him and then joined him at his home, how they had a daughter, and visited her parents in their home village. She then writes of the trauma she experienced at Xoan's death, while the daughter was away from home at a summer camp, and of her incapacity to share her sorrow with Antiia. Hence, this film confirms the centrality of letter-writing in Munro's narrative and in its screen adaptations, where letters are not only written and read, but often craved, or even intercepted and forged.

The image of Julieta in the process of writing often appears on screen (Figure 5.1). Julieta's intense voice-over reveals the contents of the letter to the audience and activates the analeptic sequences. At times (12:23–13:08; 15:15–15:50), speech operates as a sound-bridge across different shots, from the present of narration to the past of the narrative. More frequently and later in the film, Juliet's mature voice-over is superimposed upon images of the past (e.g., 30:51–31:18; 32:28–33:20). This intersemiotic and temporal dissonance (images of the past, speech in the present) is adopted in twelve scenes and foregrounds the fact that past events are interpreted and narrated through the filter of present awareness and sorrow. The letter-writing technique not only frames the temporal point of view for the film narrative. Almodóvar uses it as a filter for the expression of Julieta's interiority, thus integrating the temporal and the psychological viewpoints. As such, letter-writing takes on a therapeutic function, as it enables Julieta to overcome the silence imposed by the daughter, who will eventually write back. Paradoxically, a film Almodóvar first intended to name *Silence* celebrates Julieta as storyteller and her voice as the storytelling technique.

In order to signal leaps back and forth in the past and the time span covered by the film, Almodóvar extensively works on his

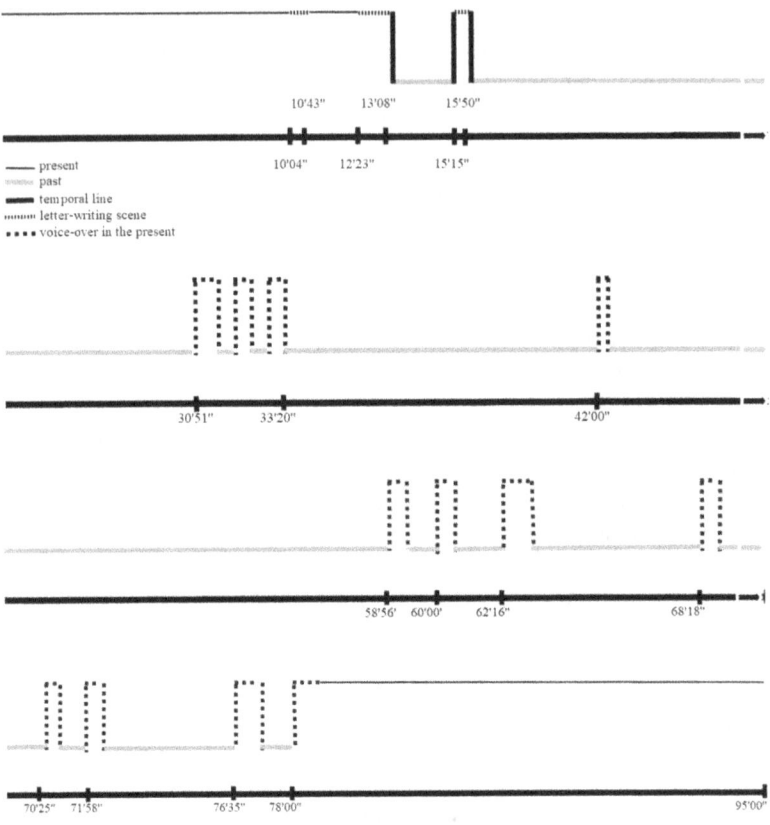

Figure 5.1 Letter-writing scenes.

female protagonist's appearance, choosing two actresses: Adriana Uguarte as the young Juliet, and Emma Suarez as the adult
protagonist. The shift occurs through a critically acclaimed cinematographic device: as Antiia dries her mother's hair, Uguarte's
face disappears beneath a towel and re-emerges as that of Suárez
(Bradshaw 2016; Kermode 2016). Moreover, both actresses change
haircut and dressing style several times throughout the film, which
marks time passing. Antiia is also played by several actresses across
the unfolding narrative: an infant, as a baby, as a child, as a young
teenager, as an older teenager.

Within the *mise en scène,* interpersonal and intrapersonal tension is often shaped through framing, lighting, and colour contrast. When Julieta is alone, lighting is generally used to express her emotional burden, in the contrast between lit and dark areas. However, when she starts writing a letter to the daughter, her room is flooded by natural sunlight coming from the outside, bringing energy and agency. Overall, the film heavily relies on saturated, intense, and vivid chromatic choices. The opening shot, for instance, shows a deep red piece of fabric, actually of a kaftan worn by Juliet while packing to leave Madrid. Colours are not used symbolically and univocally to connote a specific character across the film, but to create dramatic effects within and across the scenes. Chromatic tension is also expressed interpersonally, between characters and between the character and the surrounding setting, through the obsessive use of a blue-red scheme, used for dresses, objects, furniture items, and their mutual relationships. A similar effect is achieved through the recurrent framing technique of the two-individual shot, whereby the co-occurring characters sit or stand in front of each other. By this, the director suggests interpersonal conflict between the many characters that Juliet faces, including Antiia and Ailo (Xoan's housekeeper).

If the whole film relies on *mise en scène* and editing to express Julieta's intrapersonal grief and interpersonal conflict, the narrative releases the emotional and psychological tension towards the end. The film is, indeed, far more optimistic than the literary text in its resolution, conceiving of pain in a cathartic way (Ignjatović 2019, p. 63). The closing scene features Julieta and Lorenzo driving towards a village from where Antiia has sent a letter, informing her mother of the death of her nine-year-old son Xoan. The loss of her son, prophetically named Xoan, pushes her to contact her mother. Almodóvar's ending, thus, promises a resolution of the conflict, triggered by the tragic death, which has reminded Antiia of the loss and grief of her own mother (Keefer 2019). Keefer observes that the film's conclusion is a "somewhat happy ending" (2019, p. 46), a "happy-ish ending" (2019, p. 50). Ignjatović (2019, p. 61) has a more positive interpretation and envisages a "soothing end", bringing "hope and redemption", with Antiia "invit[ing] her mother back into her life". While Munro's text leaves tensions unsolved, mysteries blurred, and the truth ungraspable, the film offers a more concluded and conclusive piece of art. As seen in previous screen adaptations like *Edge of Madness*, it seems that the director expresses tension during the narrative at both the intra-short level and at the inter-shot level, but then achieves conflict resolution towards the end.

Making Logical Connections Clear

Letter-writing is not the only element added by the Spanish director. Absent in the Trilogy but significantly present at the beginning and at the end of the film, the character of Lorenzo Gentile offers empathy and support. Reminiscent of Ruth in *Edge of Madness,* Lorenzo balances the pervading sorrow of the narrative. In the opening sequence, Julieta abandons him without explanation when they are ready to leave Madrid and move to Portugal. Lorenzo is indeed unaware of the existence of a daughter in Julieta's life, since signs of her presence have been removed from the house. Lorenzo follows Julieta, without being noticed, in order to discover the reason behind her obscure behaviour. When he comes back to Madrid, he tries to find her again and is present when she has an accident on a street she crosses without looking at the cars around her. While she is hospitalised, he finds a picture of Julieta with Antiia and understands the secret behind Julieta's silent grief. The film closes with Lorenzo, caring and supportive, driving Julieta to reach Antiia's house.

Keefer highlights the substantial discontinuity between the literary and cinematographic texts in the logical connections between some of the major events, whose causality is explicit in the film but more elusive in the Trilogy. To illustrate her point, the Canadian scholar provides two examples (2019, p. 43). The first one appears at the beginning of the film: Julieta and Xoan make love and conceive Antiia on the train when they first meet. When Julieta decides to visit Xoan, it is because she has to tell him about the child. Juliet's travel to the Canadian North, when she receives Eric's letter, is less logically consequential than Julieta's travel. It is motivated a by an emotional impulse rather than a pragmatic reason, because on the train where they had first met, Juliet was heavily menstruating, and she and Eric had only exchanged a kiss.

In this light, another element of "linearity" in the film plot can be foregrounded: Antiia's repressed homosexuality as the reason for her departure and silence. During their second chance encounter in Madrid, Beatriz tells Julieta of the profound sentimental relationship between the two girls. She also mentions the fact that she had left for New York and Antiia for the spiritual camp in reaction to their breakup. Beatriz never returned home and had established a traditional family and followed social conventions and expectations. Shocked after this confession, Julieta feels that the Antiia's silence is more a strategy to punish herself than her mother. If the Trilogy readers never know the daughter's real motivations for her departure and silence, this element in the film story makes the narrative more accessible, and orients the viewer's textual interpretation. Clearly, this motif is typical and recognisable in Almodóvar's cinema.

A similarly logical mechanism can be envisaged later in the film, in the second example provided by Keefer. In Munro, Eric's death is presented as a fatality, whereas, in Almodóvar, Xoan dies as a consequence of the quarrel with Julieta (he deliberately decides to leave with the boat in spite of the bad weather forecast). Keefer envisages (2019, p. 46) a clear cause-effect logical mechanism underlying the cinematographic development. Further elaborating on this chain of causality, Ignjatović notices that Julieta "is visibly punished for attempting to re-create herself professionally. The tragic accident that is to be the cause of death of the fisherman partner occurs only after she has decided to start working again" (2019, p. 56). As a matter of fact, Julieta had been warned against the risks of going back to work by Ailo, who represents a conservative and patriarchal mindset (Ignjatović 2019, p. 57). Intertwined with this, Keefer observes (2019, p. 46) that Almodóvar develops the motif of punitive grief in the film, and that he saw this as part of Spanish culture, so different from the North American one.

The Spanish socio-cultural system is highly developed throughout the film, enacting the transcultural migration from the Canadian context to the Spanish one. Originally, the Spanish director had planned to set the film in New York, in the English language, and Meryl Streep had accepted Juliet's role (Bradshaw 2016; Kermode 2016). Claiming that he felt uncomfortable with the English language, Almodóvar later changed his mind. He set the film in Spain (in Madrid, Galicia for the fishing village, and the Pyrenees for the retreat) and used the Spanish language. However, the film is profoundly rooted in Spanish culture, as multimodal semiotic choices reveal. Composed by Alberto Iglesias, the original soundtrack is extensive and operates as both ideationally and interpersonally. Alongside music, many artworks express the Spanish cultural tradition: all sculptures are by Miquel Navarro and *The Seated Man* in the opening scene is an art piece the film director has had at home for twenty years (Navarro's art piece substitutes

Chagall's *I and the Village*, extensively used by Munro in the Trilogy and actually owned by the writer in Victoria, first at home and later displayed in the bookshop she ran with her husband).

Overall, the Spanish director performs a process of appropriation and transformation of the Munrovian text:

- The letter-writing trope foregrounds the protagonist, conveys interiority, narrates past events, shapes perspective, holds the narrative together.
- The director's style is expressed, for example, through the use and contrast of vivid colours, or by making logical connections clear.
- Traces of the Spanish cultural system are displayed in the language, music, design, setting, mindset.

After this Spanish interpretation and recreation of a story by Munro, the negotiation of cross-cultural patterns and issues continues, in the following section, with a migration from Canada to Iran.

From Canada to *Canaan:* An Iranian Journey

Set in an exclusive upper-middle class area in Tehran, this film tells the story of Mina who, after being married for ten years, decides to leave her husband Morteza and move to Toronto (where she has been offered a scholarship by a Canadian university). Mina was Morteza's most brilliant student when he worked as a university professor. Now an affirmed architect, the man is currently building an imposing tower in the hectic and ever-changing Iranian city. He is, however, having legal troubles with a number of people who will lose their homes, set to be demolished for the new construction. Moreover, Morteza's mother is ill, and her son wants to take Mina to the Caspian Sea to visit the old woman before the day set for the divorce: he secretly believes that this visit may change his wife's mind.

A few days before signing the divorce papers, Mina's perfect plans are also troubled by other events related to her own family. She discovers an unexpected pregnancy and secretly considers an abortion. Meanwhile, her older sister Azar suddenly arrives from Germany with her sorrow and loneliness: she has lost her son in obscure conditions. The guest is left at home when the married couple leaves to visit Morteza's mother, only to discover that she has died just before their arrival; they can only attend the funeral (Figure 5.2) and

Figure 5.2 The funeral of Morteza's mother. © 2008 photos used under permission from Mani Haghighi.

greet the relatives. On the drive back to Tehran, Mina dreams that Azar is committing suicide during her absence. Upset, she leaves the car stuck in the traffic under heavy rain and runs back home only to find that Azar is fine and has spent some pleasant time with Aziz, Morteza's close friend (Figure 5.3). Ultimately, Mina tells Morteza that she does not want the divorce any longer and that she does not want to leave her country. She also decides to keep her baby.

Shot in Tehran and produced by Hedayat Film Co., this story is narrated by the screen adaptation *Canaan,* released in 2008 in Iran. Awarded with the audience prize in the international section of Tehran's Fajr Film Festival, the film is by the Iranian-Canadian Mani Haghighi, director, screenwriter, and actor, who was born in Tehran in 1969. The son of a cinematographer and a translator, Haghighi moved to Canada aged fifteen, where he received a BA in Philosophy at McGill University in Montreal, an MA in Philosophy at Guelph University, and another BA in Cultural Studies at Trent University. He went back to Iran in 2001 and became an internationally acclaimed artist who regularly takes part in international film festivals. The biosketch showcases the director's interdisciplinary and intercultural background, of particular interest to the present discussion, where cinematographic, literary, cultural, and linguistic patterns intermingle. *Canaan's* script was written by Mani Haghighi himself and by Asghar Farhadi. The music is by the French-Iranian composer Christophe Rezai, born in Toulouse. Two tracks, *Doubt* and *Mina*, are freely available on YouTube and are worth listening to.

Entitled "Post and Beam", Munro's adapted story was preliminarily published in the pages of the *New Yorker* in December 2000, to be anthologised one year later in *Hateship, Friendship, Courtship, Loveship, Marriage*. Set in an exclusive district in North-Vancouver, the third-person story revolves around an upper-middle class married couple, Lorna and Brendan, with two children. They receive an unexpected visit from Polly, Lorna's older cousin, who has spent her unsatisfying life living with her parents. Brendan is hostile to the guest, while Lorna is profoundly uneasy. Another central character in the story is Lionel, a brilliant former student of Brendan's who had suffered from a nervous breakdown and undergone damaging treatments. Lionel and Lorna feel a mutual attraction, yet mainly of an intellectual nature. During a short trip to attend a wedding with her husband, son, and daughter, Lorna is seriously afraid that Polly might commit suicide. Upon her return, she finds out that her cousin is fine and that Polly and Lionel have become very close.

Criss-Crossing Characters

Unlike other screen adaptations of Munro's stories, *Canaan* draws inspiration from the literary text, but substantially engages with its characters, events, tone, and atmosphere. Haghighi's protagonist, Mina, is an educated and ambitious young woman who longs for her economic independence and professional fulfilment. She chose not to have children and is now ready to undergo an abortion, to get a divorce, and to emigrate to Canada, where to start a new life. Munro's Lorna is, instead, a young, uneducated mother of two. She was chosen by her future husband at a wedding—where she worked as a member of the catering staff—precisely for her young age and lack of education:

> [s]he learned later that he had been on the lookout for a wife; he was old enough, it was time. He wanted a young girl. Not a colleague, or a student, perhaps not even the sort of girl whose parents could send her to college. Unspoiled. Intelligent, but unspoiled. A wildflower, he said in the heat of those early days, and sometimes even now.
>
> (Munro 2002, p. 207)

Figure 5.3 Azar and Aziz. © 2008 photos used under permission from Mani Haghighi.

Somehow, Mina's character subverts Lorna's one.

The film's characters often show traits or patterns that diverge from their literary correlates, resulting from a web of intricate relationships. Morteza and Brendan look more similar than other adapted characters, both because of their robust professional status (the former an architect, the latter a math professor) and their straightforward attitude to life. Brendan does not appreciate Polly's presence and never listens to Lorna's family stories (spectators of this film rely on dialogue to acquire information on characters and on their stories). In this snobbish attitude to his wife's family background and legacy, this character is reminiscent of Richard in *Connection,* although he does not exhibit such harsh traits. Moreover, Brendan has the same approach towards his own family: "he had turned his back on the whole Irish package—his family and his Church and the sentimental songs—" (Munro 2002, p. 189). In the film, by contrast, it is Mina who has erased the connections with her family (she has not seen her sister for twenty years; Azar was not present at her wedding) and who wants to start a new life in Canada.

Similar dynamics govern diegetic patterns. For example, in the adapted text and the film adaptation, a different character dies: Lionel's mother in the short story and Morteza's mother in the film.

Unlike Morteza's mother, Lionel's mother is yet supported by her son, who holds up a mirror for her last make-up session. Scene placement is thus of interest, since the maternal death occurs towards the end of the film narrative but at the very beginning of the literary text, in a short narrative fragment. As an introduction, it is notably featured in the film *Hateship Loveship,* with the dying woman asking Johanna for her blue dress. In Munro's text then, it is Lionel (and not Mina) who used to be Brendan's brilliant student. However, Lionel later suffered from depression, a clinical situation absent in the film. He also secretly writes poems to Lorna, who does not mention them to Brendan. Overall, Lionel is given a more central and articulated profile in the short story, resulting in a nuanced and irreducible character. Differently, his filmic counterpart Aziz is young, fit, and sociable. Always ready to listen to his friends Morteza and Mina, he is very supportive with Azar, when she remains alone in Tehran. As such, his character is reminiscent of Ruth and Lorenzo in other adaptations, in their empathy and generosity.

Azar and Polly are also divergent in their biography, temper, and development. Azar has tragically lost her son in Germany and was forced to leave the country afterwards. She enters the film narrative in an oblique way, through her own ominous voice-over at the answering machine, announcing her arrival in Tehran twenty years after she last saw her younger sister. Across the film, she slowly abandons her gloomy sadness and decides to rent a house and settle in Tehran where Mina lives. Differently, Polly is still living with her complicated family of origin, imprisoned by her sense of duty. As such, she reminds Munro's readers of Maddy in "The Peace of Utrecht", a story from the author's first collection (often defined as autobiographical). Maddy was the sister and the one who stayed at home with the ill mother, while her sister left to build her family. Polly's appearance in the story is also different, described as a woman "full of energy and sociability, kind-hearted, confident" (Munro 2002, p. 192) in the anecdotes about her youth Brenda tells Lionel. This character does not develop in the short story, and tends to remain the object of Lorna's memories, stories, or fears.

Canaan does not offer the pleasure of adaptation intended as the recovery of familiar characters. Supposedly equivalent filmic characters (Mina-Lorna, Morteza-Brendan, Aziz-Lionel, Azar-Polley) tend to problematise, revise, sometimes even subvert literary ones. Rather than the products of smooth transposition, characters in the process of film adaptation seem mutually intertwined through prismatic and multiverse relationships. To a larger extent, the very linear correspondence between page and screen is questioned and spectators are asked to trace alternative trajectories in their interpretation of the screen adaptation as adaptation.

A Disturbance, a Definite Picture, a Dream

The film opens with a slow PoV shot focused on Mina (Figure 5.4). A persistent close-up of the woman's face is followed by the shot of a dirty and stinky cloth which has clogged the drain in her stylish and immaculate kitchen. Some workers are removing the item under Mina's gaze. In the unusual beginning, the protagonist is framed as the film's focaliser and introduces the psychoanalytic motif of an uncanny item that needs to be acknowledged and coped with. In the same sequence, Morteza receives a call from his uncle and is informed of the worrying health conditions of his mother. He blames Mina: she has told the old woman about the impending end of their marriage and destabilised her. This opening scene is set in the couple's exclusive apartment, disseminated with precious artworks and displaying a portrait of the married couple.

The kernel of the literary and film narratives is the protagonist's firm belief that something terrible has happened to a close family

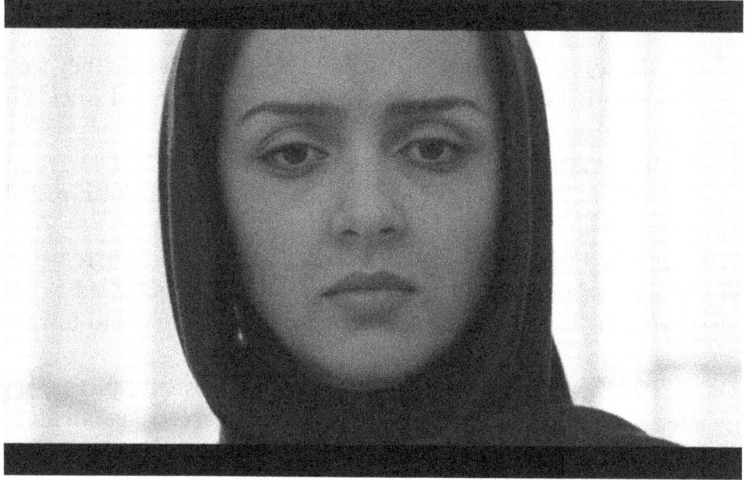

Figure 5.4 Mina. © 2008 photos used under permission from Mani Haghighi.

member. In *Canaan*, the scene is constructed as a PoV shot triggered by a close-up of Mina's face, while the woman is sleeping during the drive back home after the funeral. Evoking the opening scene as for editing, the *mise en scène* gives shape to an uncanny setting: the dark night, the heavy rain, and the deafening traffic noise. After a cut, the camera shows Mina's house, the open door on the balcony with Azar. Spectators think of a prelude to a suicide. Back at the car, Mina leaves her husband and starts running alone in the night, in a state of panic. Announced at the very beginning of the film narrative, the narrative climax unfolds at the end of an escalation of emotion and tension. After the peak, tension is released. The film ends with Mina reaching Azar at home: her sister is sitting serenely in front of a mirror. Thanks to Aziz's help, she has found an apartment for herself and she has received her luggage from the airport (it had been lost). This episode triggers an emotional response in Mina to the point that she changes her plans for her future.

In the short story, the kernel episode unfolds within a psychological dimension and does not have any concrete impact on Lorna's future life. Lorna's vision is described as a climax:

> Lorna had a faint disturbance in her mind, like a hair in her vision that could be flicked away, or could float out of sight on its own.
> But it did keep coming back. It grew more ominous and persistent, till at least it made a spring at her and she knew it for what it was.
> She was afraid—she was half certain—that while they were away in the Okanagan Polly would have committed suicide in the kitchen of the house in North Vancouver.
> In the kitchen. It was a definite picture Lorna had.
> (Munro 2002, p. 208)

Through its fractured syntax, the passage adopts an incremental approach to foreground the progressive vividness achieved by the vision (from "faint disturbance" to "definite picture") and Lorna's increasing awareness of its power.

In "Post and Beam", the "ominous and persistent" picture engenders intratextual references and leaps in time. It triggers a memory of Lorna's childhood, when she was not yet at school. Five years older, Polly had left her younger cousin alone in their grandmother's home to ride uptown and take an ingredient to the shop, a "bag of brown sugar or walnuts" (Munro 2002, p. 209). Polly had come back upset, afraid that something bad could have happened to Lorna; she was afraid that Lorna may have been kidnapped. Through Lorna's focalisation, the short story features the repetition with variation of the same event, enacting characters' reversal. This is the narrative mechanism Haghighi relies on in his screen adaptation.

Elaborated upon across the pages, the vision resurfaces again and again. Still on the drive back home from the wedding, Lorna is asked by her daughter Elizabeth to read a story entitled *Madeleine*. Lorna has left that book at home, but mother and daughter can recite the story of twelve little girls living in Paris:

> In the middle of the night,
> Miss Clavel turned on her light.
> And said, 'Something is not right'.
>
> (Munro 2001, p. 211)

Lorna's mouth gets dry and the woman is unable to continue the story. She considers praying, making a bargain, a promise, but she ignores what to offer. Although all her fears vanish when she returns home with her family, the short story keeps going back to that episode, to its emotional and psychological implicatures. Showing a technique that is both narrative and stylistic, the short story thus elaborates upon the kernel afterwards, retrospectively. In the film adaptation, differently, the ominous detail is used in the opening scene, is then elaborated upon, and ultimately leads to the climax. Hence, the night vision in the film serves as the film's diegesis, as it is followed by a release of tension and a conclusive resolution.

From Unpainted Houses to the Promised Land

As usual in Munro's stories, the title derives from an apparently trivial detail, in this case an architecture style. While admiring the area where Brendan and Lorna live, Polly refers to their building as "look[ing] like a barn". The narrator intrudes in the narrative observing that:

> She couldn't have started out worse. Brendan was very proud of their house. It was a contemporary house, built in the West Coast style called Post and Beam. Post and Beam houses were

not painted; the idea was to fit in with the original forests. So the effect was functional from the outside, with the roof flat and protruding beyond the walls. Inside, the beams were exposed and none of the wood was covered up.

(Munro 2002, p. 19)

Integrated with the surrounding natural environment, Brendan and Lorna's house epitomises an adaptive kind of architecture (which "fit[s] in with the original forest").

"Post and Beam" style in Western Canada contrasts with the tall, new buildings under construction in Tehran. The camera in *Canaan* obsessively features a vertical angle, whereby Morteza and Mina observe new buildings being constructed from the vantage point of their apartment. The privileged perspective from the luxurious residence enables them to dominate and control the surrounding area. Their approach towards architecture seems, however, dichotomic: Brendan wants to immerse into the natural environment, Morteza wants to dominate the surrounding city. Brendan is yet more problematic than his house architecture may belie. He is very "proud" of their house and likes to show his visitors the magazine article that illustrates and legitimates its value (similarly, he likes to show off his young and charming wife to his colleagues).

The Western-Canadian building adapts its architectural patterns to "fit in" with the forest it is immersed in, while the Iranian towers erase pre-existing traces. Morteza's buildings obliterate places, people, and stories. This issue is developed across several scenes revolving around the case of an old woman who has brought them to court: they meet her and then organise a meeting to resolve the problem. In this way, Haghighi seems to develop a motif Munro had addressed in "The Shining Houses", another story from her first collection. The story revolves around new white houses to be built in the place where an old farm is. The owners of the new buildings have the economic and legal power to prevail upon the farm's owner, an old woman named Mrs. Fullerton. Haghighi seems to extensively engage with Munro's work at large, especially with her early stories. While officially adapting a mature story by Munro, Haghighi may be inviting us to revisit her earlier stories, apparently less sophisticated in structure and style, but insightful in terms of themes, characterisation, and introspection.

The film's title *Canaan* may easily be ascribed to Canada, due to the phonetic proximity between the two toponyms. In this vein,

Canada may represent to Mina the Promised land, where she can forget her past and build her future. As such, *Canaan* may also evoke "the map of the Holy Land" in "Post and Beam" hanging "in the grandmother's front room" (Munro 2002, p. 191). That map was "worked in many shades of wool, showing Biblical locations" and had been offered to the Anglican Church after the woman's death (Munro 2002, p. 191). If this were the intertextual link suggested by the film's title, the name *Canaan* would yet retain the opaque and uncanny connotation it has in the Bible, and remind readers of the "wild meadow where girls were not allowed to go" (Munro 2002, p. 191) behind Lorna's childhood house, where Aunt Beatrice had probably experienced her "blotted-out disgrace", resulting in Polly's conception. In front of their houses, indeed, runs the Dye Creek, whose water was "coloured by the dye from the knotting factory" (Munro 2002, p. 191), as a persistent reminder of the aunt's sin. This line of interpretation may suggest that the Promised Land can only be reached if we honestly accept and come to terms with "the many shades" of our past and of our self.

Unlike other screen adaptations of Munro's stories, *Canaan* draws inspiration from the literary text, but substantially engages with its characters, events, tone, and atmosphere:

- Audio-visual characters often result from a web of intricate relationships among literary characters and show traits or patterns that diverge from their correlates on the page.
- *Canaan* also evokes patterns of Munro's early stories, while adapting "Post and Beam".
- The film's climax, i.e., the night vision, is followed by a release of tension and a conclusive resolution.

By this, viewers are not invited to enjoy the comfort of confirmation, but to experience the challenge of transformation.

This last chapter has explored the latest and international stage of screen adaptations of Munro's stories, specifically *Hateship Loveship*, *Julieta*, and *Canaan*. Their migration from the Canadian to the US, Spanish, and Iranian cultural, linguistic, and political systems implies the negotiation of cross-cultural patterns and issues, as well as aesthetic transformation. Overcoming linearity, equivalence, and fidelity, the adaptation process generates alternative, unpredictable, and plural trajectories of meaning-making.

References

Bodal, E., Strehlau, N. (2016) Hateship Loveship, Adaptation, in M. Buchholtz (ed.) *Alice Munro, Understanding, Adapting, Teaching*, Cham, Springer, pp. 67–74.

Bolter, J.D., Grusin R. (2009) *Remediation: Understanding New Media*, Cambridge, MA, MIT Press.

Bradshaw, P. (2016) "Julieta Review: Pedro Almódovar Ties Himself Down with Fractured Melodrama", *The Guardian*, May 17th.

Chang, J. (2013) Toronto Film Review: Hateship Loveship, *Variety*, September 8th. http://variety.com/2013/film/markets-festivals/hateship-loveship-review-toronto-1200604118/

Howells, C.A. (2009) Intimate Dislocations: Alice Munro, *Hateship, Friendship, Courtship, Loveship, Marriage*, in H. Bloom (ed.) *Alice Munro*, op. cit., pp. 167–192.

Ignjatović, S. (2019) Almodóvar's Julieta and Munro's Juliet: Beyond Cultures, in Jelena Novaković and Vesna Lopicić (eds.) *Canada 150 Filmed*, Belgrade, University of Belgrade Press, pp. 53–64.

Keefer, J. (2019) A Tale of Two Adaptations: Sarah Polley and Pedro Almodóvar do Alice Munro, in J. Novaković, V. Lopičić (eds.) *Canada 150 Filmed*, Belgrade, University of Belgrade Press, pp. 31–52.

Kermode, M. (2016) Julieta Review: Almodóvar's Five-Star Return to Form, *The Guardian*, August 28th.

Munro, A. (2002) *Hateship, Friendship, Courtship, Loveship, Marriage*, New York, Knopf.

Romney, J. (2016) Pedro Almodóvar: 'Nobody Sings. There's No Humour. I Just Wanted Restraint, *The Guardian*, August 7th.

Schuh, R. (2014) Something I've Been Meaning to Tell You: *Alice Munro and the Epistolary Mode*, Unpublished MA dissertation.

Scott, A.O. (2014) Don't Hoodwink the Help, Dear. 'Hateship Loveship', an Alice Munro Adaptation, *The New York Times*, April 10th. https://www.nytimes.com/2014/04/11/movies/hateship-loveship-an-alice-munro-adaptation.html

Thacker R. (2011) *Alice Munro: Writing Her Lives: A Biography*, Toronto, McClelland & Stewart.

Concluding Remarks

> I want the stories to keep going on, I want the story to exist some-
> where else so that in a way it's still happening, or happening over
> and over again. I don't want it to be shut up in the book and put
> away.

In an interview to Watchel (1991, p. 292), Munro seems to encourage
adaptations of her stories as forms of survival ("I don't want it to be
shut up"). The verbs she adopts invite migration ("exist somewhere
else") and ceaseless retellings ("happening over and over again"). Acknowledging the author's longing for story retelling, *A Multimodal
Stylistic Approach to Screen Adaptations of the Work of Alice Munro*
has addressed television and film adaptations released across the
last five decades. The diachronic process of adaptation has followed
a geographical trajectory from a national to an international horizon, whereby a centrifugal force has been identified, that governs
the direction, production, and fruition of the audio-visual artefacts.
Told and retold across multiple pathways, Munro's stories are constantly codified, recodified, and decodified, generating plural and
interconnected dynamics of continuity and discontinuity. Such (dis)
continuity encompasses medial and modal semiotic systems, as well
as socio-cultural, economic, and political issues.

A first group of Canadian works has been produced by or with
the support of the Canadian Broadcasting Corporation and/or of
the National Film Board of Canada. Aimed at the promotion of the
Canadian literary heritage, this early stage of screen adaptations
seems to illuminate the patterns and themes of the adapted short
story. The literary text is not only carefully transposed, but often
made explicit in its narratorial patterns and dynamics, including
narrative stance, focalisation, temporal dimension, and plot development. For example, editing techniques like the alternation

DOI: 10.4324/9781003183846-7

of interior and exterior scenes in *Boys and Girls* transduce the expression of polarised and gendered space in the short story. In *Connection*, the voice-over clarifies the narrator's status and position within the short story. In this backwards orientation, the film adaptation tends to be rather faithful to the adapted work.

Further stages of the process of screen adaptation still include "made in Canada" works; yet these are produced outside the CBC context, and are increasingly appreciated by an international audience. Directors of this mature Canadian stage tend to develop an independent aesthetic and cultural project in relation to the adapted work, with which they seem to enact a critically intracultural engagement. For example, Polley tends to emphasise and Wheeler tends to problematise the Canadian cultural context. Thus, *Away from Her* features a wide range of multimodal and multifaceted markers of the Canadian cultural heritage, also in opposition to the US cultural system. *Edge of Madness,* instead, relies on setting change, as well as the inclusion of the Aboriginal character of Ruth, to articulate a political discourse within nineteenth-century Canada, by showing tensions between Eastern and Western Canada, between minority groups and the anglophone power.

The last group of films marks the established international dimension of the adaptation process, in terms of production, direction, and fruition. With the exception of *Hateship Loveship* whose American context is never foregrounded, later works display a profound transcultural component as an element of discontinuity, that is, they rely on the new socio-cultural context for their meaning-making. Both Almodóvar and Haghighi devote specific attention to soundtracks (original in both *Julieta* and *Canaan*), interior design, exterior shooting, to highlight the new cultural context. Moreover, directors adopt various semiotic resources and strategies proper to cinematographic discourse, in order to provide their own interpretative/expressive key to the story, as in the case of Almodóvar's colour saturation and colour contrast in *Julieta*. The chromatic solution seems to primarily reflect authorial preference rather than engagement with the adapted work.

Among a range of modes, the voice-over seems to clearly demonstrate the centrifugal force governing the story of adaptations of Munro's stories, as its use is progressively reduced or becomes more specialised. In early films, the aural device was used extensively and pervasively across the whole narrative. Tending to reproduce the adapted text verbatim, numerous voice-over units seem to quote and to give voice to Munro's text. Thus, the voice-over signalled and marked a fil rouge between adapted text and adaptation (e.g., *Lives of Girls and Women*). In recent films, the voice-over is adopted more sparsely and takes on a specific function (e.g., *Edge of Madness*), related to raising a distinct issue (e.g., *Away from Her*) or enacting a particular narrative effect (e.g., *Julieta*). Moreover, it is generally used in passages which exhibit discontinuity with the adapted text, like the reading of scientific passages about Alzheimer's in *Away from Her* or Julieta's writing letters to her daughter in Almodóvar's film. Notably, both these passages do not find an equivalent in the adapted text. It seems, then, that in more recent films the voice-over is used to signal discontinuity with the adapted text, or, better, to mark the film's own aesthetic value.

Hence, changes in the adaptation process have not been regarded as expressing a betrayal of the adapted text, but as part of the adaptation process, and as being motivated by economic, medial, aesthetic factors. As such, they are not dismissed in this volume as forms of violation but are addressed as multiple semiotic patterns. Several films show how titles change: film titles become generally shorter (e.g., *Julieta*), dramatic (e.g., *Edge of Madness*), melodramatic (e.g., *Away from her*) and memorable (e.g., *Hateship Loveship*). These renamed titles may sound odd to Munro's readers, who are more familiar with the elusive solutions, marginal key-words, and intertextual echoes the adapted author had to defend during the editorial process. Only apparently a trivial phenomenon, renamed screen titles seem to express adaptation in its biological connotation, implying mutation to fit the surrounding environment. In this case, environmental conditions are constraints imposed by the production and distribution markets, the costs of the cinematographic industry. Conciseness and sentimentalism, specifically, appear a good formula for the financial success of a cinematographic product, as they favour the film's visibility, memorability, and circulation.

Alongside film names, character names are sites of change in the adaptation process. Some directors have given a name to unnamed protagonists and narrators (e.g., Margaret in *Boys and Girls* and Maureen in *Connection*), which confers vividness and tangibility to the character. This phenomenon may be related to the medium, to the audio-visual signifying system which entails a multisensorial form of fruition. In foreign films produced in later stages, place names and character names are unsurprisingly part of the transcultural process, and express the culture of the adaptation context, like Iran or Spain. Lorna and Brendan become Mina and Morteza, while Juliet, Penelope, and Eric become Julieta, Antiia, and Xoan.

Only in the case of *Thanks for the Ride* have characters' names been changed in an early Canadian work: Vicky for Lois, David for Dick, LoreAnne for Adelaide, whereas George is confirmed. The unusual solution may be seen as expressing the need to produce an independent work, albeit with an overall faithful product.

It is, however, at the level of narrative composition that most adaptations actively engage with the adapted text, with some additions (*Boys and Girls*), omissions (*Connection*, *Lives of Girls and Women*), and, most frequently, reordering (*Hateship Loveship, A Wilderness Station, Away from her*). Often, omissions affect secondary or marginal characters like Uncle Benny in *Lives of Girls and Women*, a process performed for the sake of cohesion. If Munro often gives space to bizarre characters who do not fit, directors tend to look for characters at the service of the film's diegetic system. The phenomenon of addition is rarer. In the cases of profoundly tragic or violent plots, however, some directors tend to add a supporting and caring character to temper the negative tone of the film, like Ruth in *Edge of Madness* or Lorenzo in *Julieta*. The addition of recurrent visual metaphors, as in the case of the car in *Thanks for the Ride* and of the typewriting machine in *Lives of Girls and Women* seems to serve cohesive functions. As anticipated, a significant change is the order of event presentation. If *Hateship Loveship* reorganises the material to pursue a more linear narrative, *Julieta* anchors the story on a present-tense core, from where memories are enacted, unlike the sequential unfolding of Munro's story. *Edge of Madness* is similar to *Julieta* in structure, but the solution derives from engagement with a highly fragmented epistolary text. Changes related, without being limited, to beginnings and conclusions sometimes enable the director to achieve an effect of circularity, which confers cohesion on the narrative text. Wheeler's film, for instance, open and closes with the protagonist Annie: desperate in a snow storm at the beginning, and merry at a wedding party in the end. The circular "happy ending" makes the film achieve resolution, sustain text fruition, and tempers the pervading violence. A similar technique can be identified in *Boys and Girls*.

Adaptations, especially the most recent ones, tend to provide explanations, conclusions, solutions to unsolved and open Munro stories, thus changing logical mechanisms underpinning adapted texts. Sometimes, the films provide explanations for what is vague and remains unexplained in the short story, like the case of Antiia's repressed homosexuality motivating her departure in *Julieta*. Beginnings and conclusions seem to be a privileged site of diegetic change and resolution. Beginnings are often added as a prologue (e.g., *Lives of Girls and Women*), to provide ideational information on the characters or on the socio-cultural situation, as well as to position the narrator. Conclusions are often added to solve conflicts and to close the diegesis (e.g., *Julieta*). Interestingly, this concern with story endings echoes Munro's own constant mutation of her own conclusions. In her case, however, this is motivated by resistance to closure.

In order to achieve cohesion, Almodóvar adds the pivotal scene of letter-writing as the trigger that enables the protagonist to elaborate upon her sorrow and find a connection with her daughter. Interestingly, in Munro's Trilogy, letters play a less important role, mainly as part of the diegesis. What Ailsa Cox defined as "a favourite Munro device" (Cox 2004, p. 79) seems to be significant in the whole story of Munro's adaptations. Waiting for letters is the theme of *How I met my Husband,* where Edie waits for the letter promised by the charming pilot Chris every single day and ends up marrying the postman himself. The fact that a personal letter is intercepted is followed, in *Hateship Loveship,* by the creation of a fake correspondence, and, in *Edge of Madness,* by the resolution of the murder mystery. If, in the literary texts, letters seem to operate more as textual products, in the film adaptations, they make meaning within a process of correspondence. By this narrative tension, epistles question the (dis)continuity between adapted texts and adaptations.

The relation between the adapted text and the adaptations is epitomised by the mirror, a semiotically layered and complex trope used in all film adaptations. The mirror is used by characters like Maureen in *Connection* or David in *Thanks for the Ride* in its validating and narcissistic function: to reflect, duplicate, and confirm the mirroring subject. Elsewhere, it is adopted to suggest introspection and meditation, when characters like Margaret in *Boys and Girls* or Vicky in *Thanks for the Ride* sit down and indulge in introspection in front of a mirror. Differently, some mirror scenes feature a tension between a mirroring subject and a different mirrored subject. In *Lives of Girls and Women*, the mirror inscribes conflict between mother and daughter, while in *Canaan*, it problematises the relation between two sisters. Similar functions are fulfilled by rear mirrors in *Away from her, Thanks for the Ride*, yet with a slightly different connotation of control by male gazers. In such scenes, consonant or dissonant music is generally used to project feelings, emotions and, sometimes, to anticipate narrative twists. Far from a reduplicating surface, the mirror becomes a heterotopic space, which disturbs the setting, inscribes tension in the mirroring subject, and upsets the narrative. Thus, conflict can be expressed intratextually (e.g., within and among characters), intersemiotically (i.e., among modal systems), and intertextually (i.e., among adaptations and adapted texts).

Just as the mirror does not confirm the mirroring character, the screen adaptation does not duplicate the adapted text; it rather projects multiverse prismatic trajectories. The Prologue in *Hateship Loveship* evokes a similar strategy in "Post and Beam" rather than following the story it adapts (which starts in *medias red* with a completely different scene). A similar scene is also present in Munro's "The Bear Came over the Mountain", which offers information on the protagonist's family background and the beginning of the relationship with her husband. Interestingly, the two screen adaptations by Polley and Haghighi do not deploy this solution; in *Away from her,* the fragment appears, as an embedded flashback, in a later section of the film. A similar discourse may be envisaged at a thematic level, whereby *Canaan* projects echoes of "an ealy story by Munro, "The Shining Houses", while adapting a later story, "Post and Beam". In the same vein, two characters in the Iranian film borrow traits and patterns from non-corresponding characters in the same short story (Morteza and Lionel). Overall, the adaptation process of Munro's stories seems to progressively challenge linear and confirmatory transpositions.

This line of interpretation of screen adaptations of Munro's stories is of course subjective, and derives from a personal perspective, in terms of interest, background and toolkit. It has been inspired by the appreciation of Munrovian art as constant storytelling and retelling, as an endless echoing of previous fragments and patterns. Hence, as Jellenik argues (2017, p. 44), subjectivity is unavoidable in the hermeneutics of adaptations: "The existence of adaptation *as* adaptation has more to do with the critical act of reading than it does with the creative act of writing. Adaptation […] is a critical construction". Awareness of the role of cinematographic strategies in the film adaptation process seems to sustain a critical approach to a phenomenon which involves our personal and social meaning-making of stories and storytelling.

References

Cox, A. (2004) *Alice Munro*, Tavistock, Northcote.

Jellenik, G. (2017) On the Origins of Adaptation, as Such: The Birth of a Simple Abstraction, in T. Leitch (ed.) *The Oxford Handbook of Adaptation Studies*, op. cit., pp. 37–52.

Watchel, E. (1991) An Interview with Alice Munro, in L. Spalding, M. Ondaatje (eds.) *The Brick Reader*, Toronto, Coach House, pp. 288–294.

Index

Note: **Bold** page numbers refer to tables; *italic* page numbers refer to figures.